Dedication

I dedicate this book to all mentors and masters I met, and Edouard Charles my grandfather, for giving me the thirst to search deeper in me, my teachers, such as teachers Mr. Eteve and Mr. Aubac, coaches Patrick Snow, Eric Widney, who gave me self-confidence and saw value in me, and the authors who have managed to elevate my mind such as David R. Hawkins, Deepak Chopra, Alan Cohen, Jack Canfield, and so many others. Speakers who have also made me search deeper in my values such as Les Brown, Wayne Dyer, Rev. Michael B Beckwith, Mike Dooley and Bob Doyle, among others. And to my wife and her patience, who let me write this book despite the burned food, the forgetting to buy milk and take the trash out, and all the other tasks I was supposed to do and got to do only very, very late.

The Art of Getting:

Getting What You Want, When You Want It!

Easy Steps to Change Your Life

Emrick Garam

BEST YOUR LIFE

Simple Steps to Change your Life

by Emrick Garam

www.bestyourlife.com

Table of Contents

The Art of Getting: Getting What You Want When You Want It!

By Emrick Garam

Emrick Garam

Acknowledgment

I want to thank all the speakers, trainers, authors,
And other masters of the Law of Attraction,
aka Law of Co-creation.
For giving me the inspiration to write this book.
There are so many names to mention, But in particular, thanks to
Jack Canfield, Wayne Dyer, Nan Akasha,
Joe Vitale, Deepak Chopra, Rev. Michael Beckwith,
I hope, with the help of all these people,
To make an impact in your life.
May you live in a transformed
Life with a positive energy
And bring to the world a treasure
You have forgotten for so long:
You! with your long awaited talent!
Love and Happiness to You, Always.

~~~~~~~~

Cherish the Secrets from this book.

Pass on the Secrets of this book.

Thank You

Introduction

Do You feel unhappy? Unfulfilled? You missed your chance in life? Do you feel struggling, overwhelmed? Do you feel you deserve more in life? Do you feel swimming against the tide? Do you feel your friends are getting more from life? Then this book is for you.

You have the right to be happy. This is something you need to know and to tell yourself. Happiness is not a random distribution to this one or that one. It is something that one must claim as his or hers. Happiness and success don't happen because of beauty, background, or any other circumstances. Happiness has nothing to do with luck, because luck is random. Happiness and success don't happen to hard working people either, otherwise there would be a much greater number of rich people, and most of your neighbors on your street would live in mansions and drive luxury cars instead of what they drive. Happiness is not based on wealth. Some very poor people are happy... But that is not about what we are going to talk about here.

They are there and you are here, reading this book with the hope that you will be happy and successful.

Here is good news for you, "you will be happy and successful, once you apply some of the techniques in this book. Guaranteed." This book is loaded with them. I am a practical kind of person, and I believe in practical information.

You see, I am not here to solve the problems of everyone worldwide. I am here as your guide, and by the end of this book, I hope you will see the light at the end of your tunnel, the answer to your struggles, and the life that I call the "Best Your Life" kind of life. I experimented and chose what worked best.

Actually, I have to give you a warning... This book may "blow your mind", but maybe displease you. It will depend on what is your stand about your beliefs.

...What/who do you believe God is? What do you believe Universe is? Do you believe the Universe respond to people or is a giant coincidental event that may blow into another "Big Bang" any day?

So now you can relax and enjoy this book. Pay attention to the Practices to do. Your life is about to make you spin in your shoes. You are born to live a wonderful life, which is beyond your imagination, at *this very moment. Soon you will know all what you need to live a rich, fulfilled, love filled, abundant life.*

Now. Don't thank me for that book. I am just a messenger and my job is writing these words.

Give thanks to God-Source-. To Universe, everyday.

I wish you Love, Abundance, Harmony, and Happiness.

May this book bring you all that, and much more. The Author

~~~~~

Chapter 1
Overcoming your Limiting Beliefs

"Whether you believe you can or cannot, in both ways you are always right." Henry Ford

Belief and Animals

There is a story that says that if you put a flea several days in a jar with a lead, it first will try to escape and bang its body on the lid, and then it will resign itself and stop trying. What if you open the jar? The flea would jump no higher than the lid level, and will not escape anymore.

The same principle goes for an elephant raised in the circus. First, when the elephant is a baby, the keeper would chain one leg an iron spike. First, the young elephant would struggle and try to escape. Then, when the keeper sees that he gives try and escape, the young elephant would be attached still on the same leg, with a simple rope to a wooden spike and he would not even try to escape, thinking that the rope is a chain and the stick is still made of metal.

Looking Around You

Take a minute and look around you. Look at your home, look at your furniture, your clothes, your television set, your stereo, your rugs, your garden, or patio, your car. All his is not coming out just from you; it is given to you. It is given to you by Source (aka the Creator, God, Universe), because you asked for it, you wanted it, you aimed for it, or because you visualized it. Naturally you did co-create this, but along with God-Source-Universe. You did not create all that or make anything happen just by your own will. You were helped by a Loving Creator, Source.

Hey, Can I Do This Alone?

Ab-so-lu-tely not! If you tried it alone, you would never have got all that what you have, and achieved all that what you did achieve. Just the same as God-Source gave you your body, your face, and your personality. You could not have created it all by yourself! No way! (Note: Just for all of that, you should already be grateful).

Are There God-Source Favorite Ones?

The day I lost my job, I felt like screaming in the street, to God~Source, "Why me?" I was wandering in the streets like a lost soul going back to my apartment. Then I arrive at my place, barely looking up, with a blues that can blow all candles you may lit in front of me.

I was moping around, brooding like there was not tomorrow, watching funny things on television which barely made my lift an eyebrow. I was not feeling like to eat, having no feeling to do anything fun at all, and always thinking what a failure I was.

At some point, I was listening to that little negative voice in my head telling me, "You see? I told you over and over again, you are nothing to them! And maybe you are just nothing at all! You don't know how to stand up for your rights! You don't know how to work properly! You messing up everything, and then one day your boss tells you that you have to be let go. I told you so!"

This is what many people think whenever there is a problem or a challenge coming up. If you take literally, you are asking a question, which you may never know the answer. Many ask, "So, Do God-Source has favorites?" Nope! No one. God-Source says, "There is no such thing as these are my children and those are not; so to those I'd decide: they will go and burn in hell! What? Of course not!"

God is not some judging man with a bunch of punishments or plagues, ready to throw them to anyone! Those makes good blockbuster movies, but, let us get real here... The irony is that God-Source gives to the believers as to the non-believers, the same chances, blessings, bliss, paradise on earth place, yes the atheists, the non-believers.

Even though I think they are not completely non-believers; they may call God-Source, the Creator, the One, the Lord of Everything, and so on... Why does God-Universe give to all the same chance, blessings, and great life? Because God is loving and caring, and never never says "no." God-Source loves all of us, has no preferred ones, favorites, etc. To the Creator, everyone is as precious as to the next person. God-Source doesn't judge anyone to be good or bad. We are all born the same, children of the Creator, with no difference to Him.

But, Why Do Some Receive More Than Others?

Indeed, Source, Universe, God gives naturally more to the individuals who are actually "working " on themselves, to be a better human being, those who are generous, compassionate, giving, caring, and who regularly try to help others human beings. But that doesn't mean that Source or God prefers some people over other people. Not so.

As a general rule, the God-Source gives more to the people who give, and less to the ones who keep. Why is that? You may ask... logical is the answer. He gives more to those who give more, and since they give, Source supplies more to giving people. While for those who keep, since they keep whatever they have, Source doesn't need to give to them. So Source does not. Just simple and logical.

"Ask and you shall receive.
"Seek and your shall find.
"Knock and it will be opened unto you."
The Bible

All these words drawn from the Bible
are accurate representations of the divine nature of
God-Source-Creator.
He is there, watching over us. Always.

~~~~~~~~~~~~~~~~

List Here Your Limiting Beliefs:

_____

_____

_____

_____

_____

_____

_____

_____

_____

_____

Chapter 2
Creating Your Life

"Don't die with your music in you." Wayne Dyer

Creating Your Life with God-Source-Creator-Universe

There's one thing you need to realize: you are not alone. You have someone on your side, all the time, ready to help you realize any dream and wish you may think of. You can call Him/her any way you want, I will call Him/her, God-Source-Universe.

Creating is not only a process of thought. It is energized with feelings and emotions. It is important to see the difference between your thoughts and emotions. If you only think about your wishes, or what you want without injecting the corresponding feelings or emotions into it, there will be two outcomes.

One: it is not going to happen or two: it is going to take a long, long time to come to your reality. And this is because you don't have your vibration match, your energy in alignment with your wishes.

All your experiences, people, events, possessions, you attracted them not only with a thought but also with your feelings and emotions. In other words you are not a victim of circumstances; you have created them with your thoughts and feelings.

> *"All what we are is the result of what we have thought."*
> Buddha

So now, you know. It is not a book about dwelling in the past; it is a book about you changing your life. So let us take control of the Here and the Now. The past is history, nothing we can do about it. The future is written with the present, and therefore not here yet. So, all you have to do, is to take charge and live, and act in the present, in the here and now.

Today, you are the result of your thoughts and feelings of your past.

James Arthur Ray said, "People see their current state of affair and say "this is who I am." This is not what you are; this is what you <u>were.</u> You see if you look at your current state of affairs right now, for instance you have little money on your bank acct. that is not who you are; that's the residual outcome of your past thoughts and actions."

Tips and Ideas for Practice

Think from the end. Concentrate of your goals already accomplished.

Keep your inner voice, your inner talk targeted on good results.

If any negative thought comes about, replace it with a positive thought.

Stop judging yourself and others.

Stop getting offended.

Meditate and Appreciate

"If you change the way you look at things,
The things you look at change."
Wayne Dyer

Meditation

Meditating is the act of getting the turbulent thoughts out of your mind, and to replace them with quietness, serenity, and harmony. It is a good habit for your mind, and also to attract more happiness and peace in your mind. It is like passing the vacuum cleaner in your mind and empty out the room, then to place in harmonious way beautiful non obstructive furniture which brings peace in the room of your mind.

Contemplation

It is the act of being aware of your surroundings and really, deeply enjoy what is happening around you. For instance, you may go to your backyard or a public park, and look attentively at the life developing itself around you; the beauty of flowers and their colors, a squirrel scattering in the trees, the birds singing their happy songs, the color of the grass, your pet running around or coming happily to you, the smile of a mother to her child, a great laugh between several friends, an act of kindness, a father taking the hand of his child, or picking up his child and putting him or her into his arms, and so on.

Appreciation

This is the act of thanking God-Source-Universe, and your spouse, member of the family, or friends. Appreciate is also to say something kind, and not to take anything for granted. To your spouse, to your child, you could say for instance, "Thank you for doing this, I appreciate that you are doing this, No one else that do this as well as you do, this is so sweet of you, this is so nice of you," and so forth. Then you can give him or her a hug. To your friend, you can say the same kind of word, and a tap on the shoulder.

<u>**Gratitude**</u>

It is like the sister of appreciation. If you are in a state of constant gratitude, you will find your day flowing in a joyful, harmonious, and/or a peaceful way. Do you remember a day where everything fell in perfect place and seemed to go in just the best possible way, that you felt you were in "the flow?" Most of the time, it is due to a state of thankfulness, of gratitude. You were in just the right attitude to be receiving all the blessings and gifts the life has to offer. You were in the gratitude attitude.

****

"Your Wish is my command."

"Your Wish is my command,"
Said the Genie to Aladdin.

How about you being Aladdin, and the Universe being the Genie?

Have you ever given a thought about it?

Yes, this is exactly so. Ask-Believe-Receive. If you ask what you want, and believe it will come, and then make yourself ready to receive, you will have whatever your wishes are, to your heart content.

The secret: be detached from the outcome.

Say your wish, then release to the Universe,

Allow God-Source-Universe to

Bring your wishes to reality.

~~~~~~~~~~~~~~~~~~~~~~~~~~~

"... and the Universe is going to re-arrange itself to make your wishes happen for you."

Joe Vitale

~~~~~~~

**"Your thoughts and feelings
create your life."**
"Ask - Believe - Receive"

~~~~~~

List Here what you are grateful for :

_____

_____

_____

_____

_____

_____

_____

_____

_____

_____

_____

_____

_____

_____

Chapter 3

Mastering the Law of Attraction: Using Your Energy

~~~~~~

"Many people look for their happiness in what they will have, what they will do, what they will experience.
But they have it backwards.
Happiness is not on the outside world. It is inside of you.
When you start experiencing happiness, you will attract whatever You want just like by magic!"
Marci Shimoff

~~~~~~

Practice Time: Making a List

One way to master the law of attraction is to be thankful, or grateful for what you already have. Take a piece of paper and pencil. Make a list of all what you have, all what you did, and all what you have been to reach where you are in this point in life. Soon, you will not believe of how many possessions you already have, and the amount of things or events you already accomplished. Remember not to take anything for granted.

Just list all the improvements in your life in the last 5, 3, 1 years, and then contemplate where you arrived. That is where you will start to feel grateful. And this is exactly where you want to be emotionally, charged with positive emotions and high energy vibration.

Make your list here:

_____

_____

_____

_____

_____

Seeing & Feeling Your Desires/ Goals

Whenever you start writing about your desires, or goals, write as many details as possible. For instance, do not write I want a Mercedes, but write: I want a new metallic royal blue convertible Mercedes-Benz CLK-class CLK500. Go for it!

Also, put emotions into your scripts. Visualize with emotion. For instance, write: I feel overjoyed, relaxed, and free as I drive my convertible Mercedes-Benz CLK-class CLK500. As a matter of fact, even you can't visualize, i.e., you cannot picture your Mercedes, just imagine, feel, and feel your emotions when you experience what you want to happen. For instance, I feel free and fulfilled as I drive my royal blue Mercedes convertible, and I feel the breeze on my face, as I accelerate. I hear the powerful engine smoothly revving, I feel its power as I put my foot on the gas pedal. I feel and smell the interior leather and feel the smooth leather covering the steering wheel with my hands, I hear the upbeat music on the stereo,

That is the essence of the realization of your desires. A very important detail; always write your script in the present.

~~~~~~

"You can start with nothing.
And out of nothing, and out of "no way," a way will be made."
Michael Beckwith

~~~~~~

Example – Practicing a Script

Here is a script as an example: before a challenging meeting,

Just visualize a good old friend standing right by your side.

Then, say to yourself "I am sitting in a meeting with people

from the management department.

The meeting is going just fine. Resolutions happen perfectly.

I am calm, collected, and self-assured. I know I am not alone.

My life creation partner is right by my site, and gives me complete self-confidence.

I am thankful for the way this meeting progresses. I know that I have complete control.

I am unafraid, and absolutely trust that the best solution works in my benefit.

Thank you, God-Source for your kind help."

<u>Same Vibrations:</u>
<u>"Likes attract Likes"</u>

Try this: Go to a piano and sit in front of it. Depress quietly the middle C key (in the middle of the keyboard), and play another C Key. Listen carefully. You will hear another C sounding; even you did not play it. The one who was not played is vibrating (in harmony, or harmonic), because both frequencies are really the same; i.e., their vibration rate is: 261 Herz or vibration per second. You can try this with two C keys if you want. If you don't have a piano, you also can try this on an acoustic guitar or classical guitar. Make a C on the bass string, then, play another C. You will hear the other string, you even can see them vibrating, if you pay close attention to the strings!

Try to feel them with your index finger; you even can sense the harmonic vibrating at the same frequency. The Indian sitar is entirely based of harmony strings vibrating in harmonics while not played, sounding in sympathy with the strings being plucked. A last experiment: Play a note on one instrument (e.g., on a piano) and listen to the other instrument (e.g., a guitar) you will hear the second instrument note sound in response to the other, because of the same frequency, or vibration.

This proves a point: likes frequencies makes other likes frequencies vibrate, or likes attract likes. This is a physical illustration of how energy (sounds) creates likely frequencies to vibrate together in perfect harmony, just by travelling through the air or the wood.

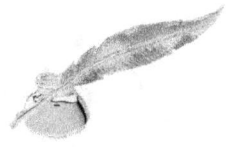

The Power of the Written Word

In the epic movie, the Ten Commandments, the pharaoh and his son said, "So Let it be written, so let it be done!"

Have you ever wondered about this? This is one of the most powerful words ever said. The job of an Egyptian Scribe was to record in writing all spoken word from the pharaoh's mouth, the life of a Pharaoh and the spoken desires of the Pharaoh. His aspirations were written (with all the attraction power within it) in a form of a record, so to magnetize and attract the wished events in his life. That is one of the great secrets of the powerful men and women in Egypt, but this happened also in other times and countries. Of course the desires were written then re-read by the pharaoh with the power of visualization and feelings. They knew the power, the energy, and the creative power of the written word. This is one of the oldest secrets. As you can see, there is nothing is new under the sun! They knew, a long time ago, that writing things had power. The power to make wishes and desires a reality.

A Practice

Someone said, "What you think about, you bring about." Whatever you say, you tell, you re-tell, you watch, you feel strongly about, you bring more in your life. Have you ever noticed that if you pay attention to a certain type of car, you will see more of that car on the road? Believe it or not, you attract these cars to cross your route, as if attracted by you energy.

Another Practice

For our purpose and to illustrate this statement, take a paper and pencil and write any number you want to attract in your life. Then notice how many times this comes into your life experience. This exercise can also be done with any various thought of color, place, people, or any idea your imagination may whisper to your mind.

The Power of the Spoken Words

Even wondered about the power of the spoken words too? It can make people love each other or hate each other. There is definite creation energy in them too! Try this experiment about the energy of the feelings. Say, "I like you" in different ways, with different feelings into it. Picture the feeling, then paint your words with the feelings, then say it out loud.

Try with these feelings: love, anger, un-carelessness, laughing, and sadness. Did you feel the difference? Did you feel the energy? That is the reason why we have to be careful with the way we say things. It is not only the words and the wording of what we say, but the energy (the feeling) that we put in our words.

By the way, this is what makes the big difference between a great actor and a bad one. They put all the feelings they have in their sentences. They know about the energy projected in their words! The audience buys it! That is also what makes an individual a great politician. Consider US President Ronald Reagan and California Governor Arnold Schwarzenegger. They are both actors! They both know about the power, the energy of feelings put into words! Even if they don't even know it, they are practicing the power of the Law of Attraction!

~ QUANTUM PHYSICS ~

Even Quantum Scientists support the Law of Attraction!

Quantum physicians and scientists have come to the conclusion, that yes, mind can bend reality. And if mind can bend reality, alter reality, and transform or shift reality, there is the evidence we have looked for: the Law of Attraction is a law, just like the law of gravity! An experiment has been conducted by quantum physicists, with a molecule accelerated in a particle accelerator.

The experiment or event was first conducted without observation and the results were recorded. Then the same experiment was conducted, but this time with an observer. By the end of the observed event, after verifying all data from the experiment, nuclear scientists have concluded the following: When an event has been observed, the outcome of the atomic particle was that its composition has been changed or shifted to a different molecular composition.

That was an incredible breakthrough. Now nuclear scientists agree that we can alter, modify, change any event (fact tested with a science experiment), only with the act of observing the event, and therefore we can come to the conclusion that your conscious mind, can change outcomes in your life.

"A simple shifting in emotion can change your entire day and your life.
If you start having a good day and let that happy feeling,
as long as you don't allow something to change your mood,
you are going to continue to attract, through the Law of Attraction,
more situations, situations, people, that maintain that happy feeling.
If you think, "I will have Good days and bad days,
or the rich get richer and the poor get poorer,"
This is the life, about what you are constantly and mostly feeling."
Bob Doyle

<u>Everything is Energy!</u>

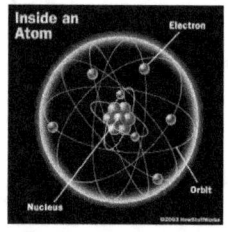

Yes, everything is energy. The Universe, the Galaxies, the stars, the sun, and then closing up to our beautiful blue planet, anything and anyone, if observed with the proper super-powered microscope, at a subatomic levels, is energy. Physicists when comparing galaxies and astral bodies, found that the same kind of systems with gravity, forces, and energy are similar to the ones found in the subatomic level.

This means that everything is made of energy. In solid, the energy or speed of atoms is slower than in liquid. Solid, liquid, gas, heat, are all composed of atoms which are vibrating at a slower rate of speed, for a solid and at a faster rate for a liquid and even faster for a gas, sound (761 miles per hour), and much faster for light (referred as "light speed", 186,282 miles per second)). Recently the speed of thought has been found to travel at 250,000 miles per seconds.

"What is Matter?"

Max Planck, 1918 Nobel Prize winner in Physics, declared in his acceptance speech: "After studying matter all my life, this is my conclusion and result: There is no matter as such! All matter originates and exists only by virtue of a force which brings the particles of atoms to vibration and holds this micro-system of atoms together. Behind this force is a conscious and intelligent mind, the matrix of all matter..."

The conscious and intelligent mind he refers to is God, the Universe, Source, and the Creator. It is by vibrating in concert with this Supreme Spirit, or the Universe, that you can co-create your reality. Whatever you want to experience, to have, to be, you can make it happen by aligning your energy with that of "the Source of all that is." You can make matter take form of anything you wish, by simply take the steps to align your energy with that of the Universe. Know what you want, Believe, and Allow the Universe to give it to you. By doing this, you create energy in the Universe, and the Universe in return will respond to your every wish.

<u>Your Goals & Your Reticular Cortex</u>

Technical – Medical Explanation about how the brain behaves with Goals. In your brain is located the Reticular Cortex, containing a Reticular Activating System. Whenever you send a goal message to it (reticular cortex), it makes you change and become more, intensely aware and alert to your surroundings, people, and opportunities to help you attain your goals. When you program your mind into achieving anything and stay focused on your goal, you act upon the opportunities coming to your awareness. Just like a self guided "missile" seeking for you to help you reach your goals. That's the miracle of your brain, and the Reticular Cortex.

NOTES:

_____

_____

_____

Chapter 4:
Mastering the Law of Attraction: Simple Steps

"It's simple. In Attraction you find the word action."Joe Vitale

The Actions

The Most Important: Be Grateful

To be grateful is an act of Love, and brings Peace and Happiness to you. This action is so much overlooked, even though it is the most important attractor factor. Whatever you see around you, you should be thankful for. Your home, your family, your loved ones, your pet, your furniture, your car, your work, your salary, your health, your legs, your eyes, your hands, your clothes.

If you are sick, you probably have at your disposition: the medication, the physicians, your doctor, your pharmacist, the insurance, the money, everything you need to get better, right? Right there, you should be grateful. If you have a car, and a decent place to live in, you should say thank you, Universe or

Source, or God. If you are over all healthy and can move about, you are blessed and should say your thanks.

<u>Practicing Being Thankful</u>

There is an exercise that Jack Canfield does in his training: he tells to every trainee to stand up, look around them, and be grateful for all what is surrounding them. The light, the doors, the rug, the carpet, the paintings, the bathroom, the decoration in the room, etc. to think of all the people involved in manufacturing them, installing them, and for their personal comfort.

Yes, you take so many things for granted. The streets which are paved, the car you drive, the bus you may ride, the police who protect you, the fire fighters who help you, the doctors who tend to you, the market or supermarket with all the good food you need for you and your family, the hospital to help those in need of intensive care, the nice apartment buildings, the nice house you live in, the nice furniture you live in, the nice clothes and shoes you have. For all of these things, well you have enough to write about! Here is a simple exercise which will help you see these good things you have in your life.

Now A word about Complaining...

Also, doing this journal or diary will help you to slow down in your complaints, upsets, or sourness in your life. So many people are complaining about any little things! Too early, too late, too much, not enough, too pricey, too cheap quality, too many of this, not enough of that! Come on, stop it already! This is a bad habit you first need to change very soon! And this bad habit is low or slow energy, which slows down the attraction process, and the creation of your ideal events in your life.

Note: Complaining lowers your energy level or vibration level.

Starting a Gratitude Journal

Also, it is recommended to start a gratitude journal or diary, where every day you will put at least 3 or 4 things you are grateful for. Take a few minutes, everyday, to first be thankful, feel it in your heart, then write down even little things you can be thankful for. A bird singing, a smile from a child, a nice word you heard, anything counts. This is very important. If you put your heart into it, it triggers a wonderful positive energy of love, gratitude, and abundance in your mind, which creates more energy for abundance, love, and wealth in your life!

"If You Want It, Give It First!"

Anecdote with Tony Robbins

Give whatever you want to get. What? You may ask. But I will give money when I have more! Well Tony Robins, at one early point in his life, had only a few dollars left. He tells that he saw this child treating his mother with so much love, and care, but didn't have any money to pay for a meal in some fast-food restaurant, that he took half of the few dollars he had and gave it to the child. The pleasure he had in giving was so great that he forgot about his own problems. And not much later, things started to really pick up for Tony! Yes, this action triggered the Universe to deliver money to him. This is all explained in the fact that energy found in service and goodness attracts more of it to the creator of good deeds.

Anything you want more of, just give away. You want to get more money? Give money! Be generous! You want to have more time? Give your time! Volunteer your time.

One thing is more precious than any money in the world: time! Look around you. 80 % of what you have you don't use. This is a good time to make some space and give away whatever you don't use. A parameter? Anything you did not use for the last 6 months should end up at a charity.

~~~~~~

"Size is nothing to the Universe. It is no more difficult to attract, something that we consider huge than something that is very small.

The Universe does everything it does with "zero" effort.
Grass doesn't strain to grow; it's just effortless. It's just this great design.
It's all about what's going on in your mind. It's about what we put in place.
If one says this is big, it's going to take more time and this is small I will give it an hour. These are our rule that we define ourselves.
These are not rules set by the Universe.
If you provide the feelings of having it right now, it will respond."
Bob Doyle

~~~~~~

Practicing: Clean Your Home

Start making the empty in your office, in your garage, in your storage room, in your attic if you have one, and /or in your shed. Start with the obvious things to give first. One box for the obvious, on which you will write: "donation"; one box for the maybe keep/maybe give. Write "Maybe Keep or Give" on it. Third box: write Storage on it plus the content Xmas decorations, etc. Then take the box(es) to donation. Where to start? I would suggest where you have the more stuff; office, garage, storage room, attic and/or basement, and then move to kitchen, bedroom(s), and living room.

Do this for 1 to 2 hours, every week-end, until you are done. Do not over do it, since will cause you to be exhausted.

Give Away Now!

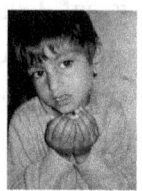

It is good to give away; good for the mind, good for your living space, and good for the ones who just needed that old stuff you are not using anymore.

Plus, it will empty the clutter which not only may upset your subconscious, but also slow down or block the good energy. The good energy need to flow freely, so it can help you to create, and it can also create for you, manifest your goals and desires.

A healthy mind in a healthy body and a healthy mind in a healthy environment.

Cleaning your home will help you clearing your mind.

Be Generous!

I know, I know ... You are already asking yourself "Why should I?"

The following may well indicate reasons why should you...

Be thankful that you can afford to be generous, to pay your bills, to pay for your gas, etc.

Whenever You Give, Be Thankful!

When you give, be thankful you can give.

This action in itself is a great blessing, or luck! That means you have enough to spare! Think of it for a moment. Where to give? In the market, there are charity drives. Give. In the street there are poor people begging. Give.

Deepak Chopra suggests something. When you give, give a silent blessing, a kind word, a smile, but give with all your heart and care. Giving with even the slightest resentment is not giving; it is just lending. The true gift is carried out by the heart, not only by the hand.

~~~~~~~~~~~~~~~~~~~~~~~~~~~~~~~~~~

"To be grateful is an act of Love, and brings Peace and Happiness to you."
To Give is also an act of Love, and brings Peace and Happiness to you.

~~~~~~~~~~~~~~~~~~~~~

~~~~~~~~~~~~~~~~~~~~~~~~~~~~~~~~~~

"Simple Kindness to oneself is the Most powerful force of all."

Following Your Passion

In an experiment, How to become a millionaire, 1,500 people were studied. They were divided into 2 groups. Group A said they would first purse their money first, and do what they wanted later. There were 1,250 people total in group A. Group B said they would pursue their interest first, and trust money would come later.

Guess what happened. Some 20 years later, 102 millionaires came from both groups. Only 1 came out in Group A. 101 millionaires came from group B. The very same group who said they would follow their passion first and worry about money afterward.

Conclusion: Be passionate! Follow your passion.

Many people make money their goal #1. But Money is not a goal by itself. It is only a mean to attain your goal!

Being Positive

No matter what and how, be positive. If you find an obstacle or difficulty in your life,

Be thankful. In each challenge there is something positive; a lesson to be learned, and the rise to the occasion makes you stronger and give you more to your character. If you fight a challenge, you will learn eventually how to stop reacting and begin responding, which will raise your energy level, and by doing so, will put you in alignment, in the same frequency as the Universe.

Also, by being positive, you will strengthen your positive belief system, which will accelerate the attraction of what you want more in your life.

~~~~~

" People see their current state of affair and say "This is who
I am."
This is not what you are; this is what you were. If you look at
your current state of affaire right now, for instance you have
little money on your bank account.
That is not who you are;
That's the residual outcome of your past thoughts and
actions."

James Arthur Ray

~~~~~

NOTES:

_____

_____

_____

_____

_____

_____

_____

_____

_____

_____

Chapter 5:
METHODS FOR ATTRACTING

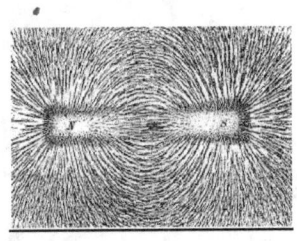

"The Law of attraction is: Like attracts like." Bob Proctor

After long research on the subject, these are the main methods for attracting. Included are several, so you can pick and choose the one that works out best for you.

The 5 Steps Method

1 Know what you don't want.

2 Select what you do want.

3 Clear all negative or limiting beliefs

4 Feel what it would be like to have, do, or be whatever you want.

5 Let go as you act on your intuitive impulses, and allow the results to manifest themselves!

Alternate method

1-- List what you don't want

2-- List what you do want

3-- Visualize or imagine what you do want with feelings and emotions.

4-- Allow Universe, God-Source to deliver it to you.

Yet Another method

Take a piece of paper and make a T chart with two columns

1 On the Left, List what you do not want.

2 On the Right, List what you want, by turning around the do Not want statement

Example:

I don't want to be careful with money, and skip going out. (On the left column)

I am happy and go out whenever I want to! (On the right column)

3 Say and Believe in your right column statements

4 Receive (Be thankful for your right statements, and say thanks)

Act Exactly As If...

After deciding what or who you would like to be, act as if you are already in the circumstances you desire right now. For instance, let's say you want to be a famous actor. Look at other actors, and their behavior, life style, how they talk, how they dress, where they go, what they buy, and even what they drive. Then, as a little child who knows how to dream, just copy them, and mimic them.

If you cannot afford the expensive car, just go and try it, and imagine that it is your car. Just "Act As If" you already have what you want, do what you want, be who you want to be, and the outer reality will match the inner reality. Remember: the brain does not know the difference between the inner reality and the outer reality. So the brain will believe what you "feed" it, and will automatically deliver it to you. By the way this aligns perfectly with the visualization on your vision board (but more on this later...)

Practicing: Exercise

Fetch your video camera and your tape-recorder or voice-recorder. Have a script ready as if you already are the personality you want to be (Mr. or Ms. known Actor, Rich entrepreneur, Successful speaker, well-known Artist, bestselling Author, or anyone you really want to be.) Rehearse your first rate speech, imagine the questions you would be asked on a TV show, Good Morning America, the View, Oprah Show, DeGeneres Show, and answer them with the same demeanor as any of the famous ones have shown. Believe that this is a training exercise that precedes the real thing, be "in the zone" and "Act As If." Very successful people have done it; Jack Canfield, Victor Hansen, Joe Vitale, and many others.

~~~~~~~~~~~

"What is your condition right now, that is only your <u>current</u> reality."
Joe Vitale

~~~~~~~~~~~

Your reality is always and ever changing. Nothing is permanent. Since everything is energy, the only thing that would permanent is energy, or God-Source-Universe. What you see yourself surrounding by, who you are, what you do; what you experience is just your current reality. You are every second, every minute, changing; want it or not. Now it is the time to decide: what do you want to change in your life?

~~~~~~

"If you continue doing what you do exactly what you been doing
and expecting a different result,
You are "out of your mind.""
Tony Robbins

~~~~~

Notes:

_____

_____

_____

_____

_____

_____

Chapter 6:
Building a Vision Board

"Create a vision of what you really want. It is the first step of Creation."

Building and Using
A Vision Board

Sample of completed Vision Book

Material:
Options for a Support

- A 3 flaps vision board made up with a 36" x 48" "premium foam display board", which you can get from your local office store (e.g., Office Depot, Staples)
- or: a 24"x 36" white card board
- or: a 24"x 36" magnetic white board
- Magnets for the magnetic white board

Visuals for Support

- Pictures or photos of what you want
- Photos of you and yours being happy
- Short Affirmations such as, I am successful, I feel Happy, I help others, etc.
- A Picture of yourself looking successful (with necktie or a pro attire for women)

Note: I use the 3 flaps vision board in the bedroom and the 24"x 36" magnetic white board in the office. I find the magnetic board practical and like it because I like to re-arrange from time to time the picture, and adding and replacing items is also a plus. Last, it takes so little time to do it, that it is worth the investment.

Using Your Vision Board

Every morning as you wake up, and evening as you go to sleep, look intensely to your vision board, and imagine yourself to be there, in the picture of the place you aim to live or visit (by the way, you can cut a picture of yourself, around your body, and affix it on the top of the place you want to be, right in the foreground).

Imagining Being There

While you are looking to your vision board, or you may close your eyes if you prefer, imagine you are there. Imagine it with all your senses, as suggested in the Neville Method*, how it would be like being right there in the picture.

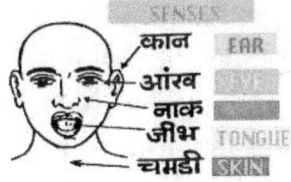

How it would look? What would you see? Think of shapes and color. What you would hear or listen? What you would smell? How the weather is like (hot, warm, mild, or cold)? Would you be eating there? What would you have? What dish and /or wine would you have? Would you be hearing your family, your friends laughing, playing, and/or congratulating you? Make this moment a firework of sensorial feelings. The more sensorial details are the better.

Wayne Dyer, speaker and author, says that each time he writes a book, he has a mock copy of his book sitting on his desk. He says and affirms that seeing the book already finished not only motivates him, but helps him writing the book with much more ease than without this model. He feels happy with his new book, before he finishes it. He anticipates the situation of having the book already put to print, and it is charged with feelings and emotions all about achievement and accomplishment.

* **Neville Goddard** was a Metaphysics teacher, who taught and lectured in the 1950s, 60s and 70s.

His ideas of "thinking from the end" and visualizing have lead to a catch phrase in "creating wealth" seminars called "Nevillizing".

Using your Feelings, your Emotions

Imagine also how would you feel once you are already in the wish come true. Would you feel happy, content, fulfilled, in love, excited, successful, wealthy? Charge your wishes with all these kinds of feelings and emotions. Doing this literally catalyze your creative process. Remember to "feel" how it feels to already have it, experience it, live it, be it.

Being in a State of Gratitude, Constantly

Be in the state of absolute belief, trust, abundance, and true gratitude. Give thanks and be really with all your heart and soul grateful for receiving this gift from God, Source, and/or Universe. Be grateful. Be thankful, for this is on its way to you. While being grateful, be sincere. This should not be a routine to just follow because it is written. This needs to be felt with all your heart and soul. "It is better to give one coin with all your heart than to give 50 with your hand."

A Note: Being Generous

Also, include a statement of how this is going to help others. This feeling is crucial. Try to include why you want this to happen. Include others in the benefits of your wish coming to reality. This notion is important, because you have to remember that nothing really belongs to us, all we have, experienced, and "are" now, are gifts from God-Source-Universe. You have to be grateful, and receive all these gifts with grace, and a vision of how you could make others benefit from it. Doing this will raise the energy to your vision of your wishes. You will be aligned with high and fast energy. If you don't include any benefit to others in your wish, this may be an act of selfishness, greed, and self contentment, or other low energy nature quality, which lowers the Universal energy, and make your wish take much longer to come to your reality.

About Wishes

When you are thinking or visualizing your wishes or goals, ask myself, "How can I help, share, love others, once my dream has come true?" True happiness happens when we find our purpose. Your purpose in this world is to find your talent, your quality, your status and make the world profit from it. Don't die with the music in you, as said Wayne Dyer. Make the world hear your own music, your own talent. I heard once, "If you don't find your talent, help others find theirs."

Note that during the Great Depression was the time of Hollywood "Golden Years" or "Golden Era." Why you may ask, because it was during that time that the world needed to dream the most, to forget about their privation, their harsh condition. Movie makers were not the only ones. Henry Ford, by then declared that he wanted all Americans to have a car per family which they all could afford. These words gave hope and courage to those who were in such a hardship.

Goals and Wishes

After you wrote your goals, It is important to read them twice, or even three times a   day. This will help set in motion, or activate your **Reticular Activating System (RAS)***, stimulate your subconscious, to start its job as a creative   partner to start finding ways to achieve your goals.

Read each goal of the list aloud, with enthusiasm, and as much feelings and emotion as possible. Then proceed to the next one.

Next, close your eyes and see yourself in, or with the goal already achieved.

Finally, feel your emotions set off by this goal, still in the presence of your wish already achieved.

Remember to read your goals list aloud twice or three times daily.

Chapter 7
This is Not Working!

"Go easy on yourself. Nature doesn't struggle, it is letting itself be. No rush, no push."

OK. Now you have done everything I discussed but you are finding yourself exactly at the same point, after several weeks. So, you may be asking yourself "Why is it not working?" with a disappointed and angry feeling. Do not worry; I am here to help you.

These are two main causes which might impair the realization of your wishes. These reasons are often co-dependent, by which one causes the other to happen.

Reason #1: Lack of Belief

Because of your lack of belief, I like the analogy of Bob Doyle in the Secret. He says that when you start visualizing your wish, it is like a seed. Some time passes, some days, then the seed starts to sprout its roots. Then some more time goes about, and the seed cracks opening the soil. More time passes, and the curled stem start to ease its way through the soil. And right at this moment, you might say, "Forget it, it is not working." And the stem, which was about to show up its tender green first shoots, goes back down into the soil.

Reason #2: Impatience

Lack of belief and Impatience are really tied in together. Maybe it is not working because of your impatience. But it is not really your fault. We live in a society where everything goes so fast, that we can't wait. Look around: people always rush. Even on Sundays! Take your time! Slow down. People are numb with impatience; with their texting others, and talking over the phone of trivial things that could easily wait.

Sometimes, using the miracle of technology, they even argue over the phone! Could this wait? I believe that if they waited a little, their angry feelings would go down, and find a positive resolve. But because of being impatient, the rushed judgments bring about unsolved issues. Impatience in the city. I live in the city, next to two intersections. One with a stop sign, one with a traffic light. Every month, there are accidents either for neglecting to stop at the stop sign while incoming cars are going (sometimes too fast, I agree), or because they make their turn too close to other coming cars (which, again may be speeding).

<u>Reason #3 Another Reason</u>

Maybe you are asking something with negation words like, Not or No in it.

This wish, such as "I don't want to miss money ever again." Is not going to work. Here is an example. I want you to not imagine ... the Statue of Liberty. What is the first thing that you imagine? The Statue of Liberty of course! You see. God-Source-Universe does not take account of all negations such as; Do Not, Not, no, never, less, fewer, etc. God-Source "thinks" only in positive. So God-Source hears "miss money" and forgets the rest. Then when God-Source hears that, God-Source delivers more of it, since each thought, especially charged with strong emotion is energy. In this case, try to say,"I always have more money that I need." There; you don't see any negation; therefore it will work like a breeze.

<u>Reason #4 Not Using the Present Tense</u>

Ah! That is another glitch to your wish. Let say that you say in your affirmations, "I will be living in a mansion, someday." So, it is not working. Why, you ask, because your affirmation says, "I will..." Then God-Source hears. "I will..." and delivers you the notion of future. Do you know the theory that an arrow will never reach a target? Because it will go half way, then half of half way, then, half of half of half way. It will go! Get it? It WILL go. Well that is the same thing with "I will..." Do you remember about energy? Here the energy is put in the words "I will" in the future tense. But if you say "I am living in a large mansion." Do you feel the difference? Uh? Uh? Oh yeah! Note: You see, the mind does not make a difference between the inner-reality (vision of reality for the future) and outer-reality, the wish come to reality already.

Adding More Details

When you say your affirmations, are you really thinking and seeing your wish with details, or is it sort of unclear? Let me explain. Let's say that your affirmation says, "I am rich, very rich." Rich is totally unclear and object to comparison, an unclear idea. Rich for one would be to make $50,000 in the US, or for another person making $100,000 and up, and so on. Note: The poorest of any working American employee salary is a rich man for a large percentage of the world population. We are considered rich, very rich to a very large number of people on our lovely planet.

Consider this: If you earn $ 12,000 per year, you belong to 12.88 % of the world working population. What if you make say $24,000 per year? Well now you are at the top 10.29% of richest persons in the world! How about if you are making a staggering $30,000 a year? Now you belong to the 7.16% richest persons on the planet. And $40,000, your position is now at the top 3.17% of the world population. How about $50,000? Well you'd belong to ... 0.89% of the entire world mankind. That makes you think... When you see these numbers, don't you feel like being grateful living in such a rich, generous, wealthy country? Don't you feel blessed in the deepest sense of the word?

<u>Ordering Fast Food</u>

Here is an example: imagine that you order a pizza. Now this pizzeria is special. It is a new shop, and right now, there is only one employee. You tell the pizza employee exactly what you want on it: pepperoni, mushrooms, and extra cheese, bell peppers, and what not. He tells you "OK, your pizza will arrive in approximately 30 minutes." 5 minutes later, you call them back and ask," Did you get my order?" Then 5 minutes later, you call them back and ask, "Are you going to deliver it soon?" Then 5 minutes later, you call them back again and ask them another question, showing them that you are really impatient to get your pizza delivered.

Honestly, do you think that a: your order is going to come faster? (Maybe not, since he is the only one working, when he answers the phone, he is not preparing your pizza). B: your order may be the last one they take c: if they take your order, maybe it will take way longer, because they do not really care about difficult customers? In any case, impatience will affect the time your order will take, if it is on its way.

This is to illustrate what mistake many are doing when asking for what they want. They do not let God-Source-Universe take the time to create. Constantly checking on your order will surely slow things down. Remember to let go, the release your wish, to leave it in the hands of God-Source-Universe and trust, believe that your wish is already in the making, in the creation process. Believe, Believe, And Believe.

<u>Maybe Your Wish Might Be Too Vague</u>

Maybe your order is too vague, and therefore inefficient. For instance, one day, during a seminar, the speaker asked the crowd, "So, what do you want?" Someone answered "I want more money!" the speaker came to him, gave him a dollar and said "Here you are; now you have more money!" The man said "no, much more money!"

Be precise of how much you want! If you want a yacht, how big, what color, how many in the crew, pilot or you will pilot your own yacht? If you want a mansion , how many stories, how big, how many rooms, and bathrooms, a tennis court, a basket ball court, a pool and How big, what shape, trees and what kind? If you want a car, what brand, model, year, color, leather, options? Do you "see" what you want, with all the details?

Make sure that your order is made with precision, with all the necessary information, so you will not be disappointed.

Here is another example to illustrate my point. There was this man who repeated for many days his affirmation and intention: "I will touch and handle millions of dollars every day." And he continued wishing and saying this affirmation, everyday, for a long while. Finally, his wish came true, and he was hired as a bank employee, and his job was to stack up bills in piles in the vault! Yes, he did touch and handle millions of dollars; it was just other people's money! As the saying goes, "Be careful with what you wish for!"

NOTES:

_____

_____

_____

_____

_____

_____

_____

_____

_____

_____

Chapter 8
Letting Go, Letting God-Source!

"In connecting and allowing, accepting and free of judging, find your way to bliss."EG

Slow down. Take your time. If someone wants to rush and cut you off on the road, let him or her go ahead. Don't fight it. People are people. See this is a different way; maybe the driver is late, or has an emergency or a crisis, and needs to be to his/her destination very quickly.

Impatience

Lots of people get into accidents because of their impatience. A piece of advice here:

Before going to drive, smile, and say to yourself; "I am a patient driver, and everybody is my friend on the road; no matter what happens." While driving, smile, relax, be positive and master of yourself. Take your time, and do not react, but respond. Be in control even if the others are not in control, out of control so to say. Do not focus on them, let them go, and feel and be happy.

"Let Go and Let God"

If you don't let go (and let God) it is not going to happen. Unless you do this, nothing will come about. There must be a moment or a certain time, where you completely relinquish all your will, your thought about your wishes.

Someone made the following analogy: Imagine a seed. You plant the seed, you water the seed, it starts sprouting in the soil; fir the root, then the germ, and then it slowly starts to grow. During this time, nothing appears. There is something happening, but it is invisible. Then, after a few weeks, finally something is appearing.

It is the same for the law of attraction or the creation process. First, you wish, you write or say out loud your desire with feelings and emotion, then you let go, you allow. Well you have to trust God-Source-Universe that it is in its way! If you don't it is like stopping watering the sprout, and it will die, and nothing is going to happen!

NOTES:

_____

_____

_____

_____

_____

_____

_____

_____

_____

_____

Chapter 9
Making No More Excuses!

"Our mission is to make this world a better place."Emrick

"To believe in yourself is an attitude."Emrick

Excuses, Beliefs Destroyers

*"Buts are the Butt of success,
the dead end of your life wishes."
Unknown*

Excuses

Saying, "I can't ..., because..."

Excuses many times start with "I can't because..." Is the beginning of an <u>excuse</u>. An excuse is "I can't because ..."

Examples: I can't run my own business, because... I am too old, I am too inexperienced, I am too poor, I am too young, etc.

Excuses are belief destroyers; you got to get rid of them! They are inner limits, undermining your best, your potential for success. Someone said once, "beware of yourself, you can be your best ally, but also your worst enemy."

Negative Self ~Talk

Negative self talk is another one. There is always that little voice in your head, criticizing you at the every occasion, many events. It goes, "Are you out of your mind? Do you know how much time/money this is going to take? Are you nuts? What is wrong with you? You can't do that! It's too much! It's too risky! It's too soon! It's too late!

And then, what do you do? You give up, finding all kind of excuses. And then one day you realize, "Oh my gosh! I could have done that; I could have taken a shot, taken a little risk and made myself and my spouse happy!" Do you want to look at yourself in the mirror and talk to yourself like that? I am sure you don't want to do that!

The B word: "but"

Excuse can be the second part of a sentence. This is another one. ..., the word "but..."

Do you live to always please others (especially your mom, dad, spouse), or do you live to reach your goals, make you wishes a reality, and be passionate about a life you know you truly deserve?

Example: I am sure I can do this (I know it!), **but...** followed by an excuse, often referring to another person or persons.

Instances

"I know to be capable of running this business; I feel like to get my pilot license, but...

"What is my wife going to say?   What are others going to say?

"What is my mom/dad going to think?   How are my friends going to react?   I am too old, I am inexperienced,

"I don't have the money, and I can't do this to my spouse, bla, bla, bla..."

Hey! Patience! Believe!

Sometime you may think you have to have this thing and that thing immediately. But this is the wrong approach. I have countless examples of where I was not rushing anything, I had my creation partner, God-Source, take the lead.

For instance, one day, I didn't have enough money to go on a boat tour. I just sat, and wish I could go on the tour. Then I meditated on how it would be just fabulous to be on the boat, observing and admiring the treasures of nature. A moment passed; maybe half an hour and guess what? After these several minutes, they let me come on board the boat and go on the tour for free!

Thanks to my partner, God-Source! Just say something like "that would be nice to ...go on this trip, that tour, etc, and let go, and let God. It doesn't fail! Don't for get to thank God-Source, and you also can do that by donating money, if you can afford it. Don't look for the opportunity; it will present itself in time!

Being in Gratitude and Smiling

"Each time I see a smile, I am grateful. Each time I hear a laugh or a bird song, I am grateful. I am aware that these simple things are miracles, and keep them inside. Then I radiate, or project my gratitude in good words and smiles to the ones who can't see them. And the miracle of awareness enlightens their minds... They become happier, and my mission is in the doing... That is my purpose in life. Make others happy..."

Something interesting happens in making others happy. Doing this elevates your inner energy, makes you happier, makes you more immune to illnesses, and attracts more happy experiences in your life. You start noticing and experiencing more and more good things in life, and it gives you a tremendous high energy and alignment with anything you do.

Making others happy makes you happier.

Try it! You will see! You will love it!

God-Source, the Power of "No"

If you have debt and say I don't want to have debt anymore! With strong feelings and emotions. Then universe hears debts. So he gives you more of it. You want to get out of debt or you don't want to be in debt, you going to get debts! So if you don't want to have debt, replace the word debt with another word, and do not use the words "no, not, never, ever, or any other negative. In this example, you want to say, "I want to be debt-free!" with all feelings and emotion.

Try this: "Do not think about the Statue of Liberty!" what was the first thing that popped in your mind? See, well, now you see. You can try with any object or place you can think of. Try that now, "Don't think about a tomato, a pitbull dog, a cat, a car, an airplane, a horse, a bear, a mansion, a tent, a park, a baby, the moon, the sun, a rocket-ship, or Washington", every time you are going to see those objects or situations appearing like magically in your mind's eye. In this case, don't think is equal to: do think. The word "No" has no effect on your wish, desire, or anything you want. To solve that, just think of the opposite word which corresponds with what you do want.

A note: When people are asked to say all the things they want, they usually think of all the things they don't want.

I don't want to fail
I don't want to struggle at work,
I don't want to work here,
I don't want to get sick,

I don't want any debts,
I don't want such a miserable bank account,
I don't want my old car,
and so on.

People are so focused of what they don't want that they forget about what they do want. From this day on, focus on what you want, and detach yourself from what you don't want. You will see a great change in your optic and feel of life in general.

Fearful, Fear

The worst state emotion is to be fearful of something. This something is precisely what you are most likely to attract. Fear is a primal emotion, from which all negative emotions stem and the most energy-charged feeling along with its counterpart, Love. So Fear is very fast to precipitate your event, for it to come about very quickly. Anyone who is afraid of something is attracting that something faster than anything else, just because it is charged with the high vibration emotion: Fear.

For example, a person who is afraid of spiders or snakes will attract situations, just like a magnet, where they will see a spider or a snake. Another example is a person who has a strong resentment or fear of a certain type of relationship, will have the tendency to divorce or separate from that certain type of relationship and find him or herself in exactly the same kind of relationship after finishing the former relationship. Of course, do not fear Fear.

The best way to eliminate Fear is to accept it, to welcome it, and then to release it, following the Sedona Method, discussed in one of the next chapters.

NOTES:_____

_____

_____

_____

_____

_____

_____

_____

_____

Chapter 10

Universal, Worldwide Beliefs: Solving Big Problems in Our World

~~~~~

"What you resist persists." Karl Jung

~~~~~

Nowadays we want to fight many major problems worldwide. We want to fight against cancer, against poverty, against drugs, against terrorism, against violence, and so on. The point is, we fight anything <u>we don't want</u>, with our emotion completely energized, usually anger, anxiety or frustration, and we are adding to the issue, to the problem.

We are adding energy to these issues and they're getting stronger, bigger, because we are creating a resistance to it. Karl Jung said, "What you resist persists." For instance, the anti-war movement creates more war; the anti- drug movement also creates more drugs. Mother Theresa understood that problem. She said, I will never go to an antiwar rally. But if you have a Peace rally, I will go." So if you want to take a position about this issue, if you are anti- war, be pro- peace.

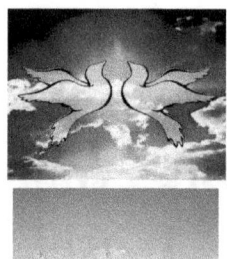

NOTES:

_____

_____

_____

_____

_____

_____

_____

_____

_____

_____

Chapter 11
Beliefs:
Believing in yourself!

"If you think you can, you can.
If you think you can't, you can't.
Either way, you are right."
Henry Ford.

Beware of Your Limiting Beliefs

The Flea in the Jar

The story goes that if you put a flea in a jar, and close the lid, a few days later, you

Open the jar and the flea doesn't jump higher than the lid. It believes

The lid is still there, because it bumped into it so many times.

So it is for your beliefs. So let's take out the lid and limitations,

And let's jump higher, as we were supposed to, anyway.

In respect to your beliefs, you have to have an open mind,
Otherwise it is simply not going to work.

God-Source wants you to succeed, be rich, be happy, and live a life of dreams. He is

Your partner for life. He is not judging anyone. He tries to help you to live happily.

He is not the punisher. Suffering and punishment come mainly from your ego.

Beliefs, Religion, and You...

About religion:

If you believe in God, Allah, Krishna, Yaveh, etc. That's Fine.

But if you believe they are going to punish you for how you create your life, beware they will!

Because that is your belief! If you believe they will punish you no matter what, they will.

If you believe an ancestor will pursue you for changing your life and your beliefs, he/she will.

Do you see what I mean? You are attracting any event in your life. God is not there to get you! God-Source loves you, even if you are the last soul on earth. He (or She) is just and simply put, pure good energy, pure Love.

Our General Beliefs

Also: In regards to your general beliefs:

You have been programmed by

Your parents, siblings, friends,

Teachers, ministers of different religions,

and unfortunately by television (programs, news, talk-shows (some are the worst))

on how to think, what to believe, how you act, how you re-act, how you behave, etc.

Well, this is the moment where I tell you:

"Beware! This "programming" may be wrong! When I say all this, I don't mean all 100%. But a great part of your beliefs is learned, acquired, put in your brain, and most of it, believe it or not through emotion such as fear, and love, and also through manipulation.

Listen many people talking:

--Life is hard ... (how about the life condition we have?

The infinite possibilities, the information we can access so easily? The means of communication i.e., cellular telephones?)

--On the News: "The economy is in crisis!".... (That is a virus of a belief that is spread around by the media; if they say something; unfortunately, many viewers are going to believe them. They say we have the experts confirming this situation; half of the experts are making mistakes! NOTE: You know who is the best expert? You! If you want to get information on whatever event they may be talking about, you can go on line and research university sites, and trusted sites, such as Wikipedia who don't try to lure you in their negative philosophy. You can read books from the library too!) The problem with beliefs is that if they are shared by many, they can alter our common reality. Since what we beliefs come about, if we believe there will be a catastrophe, it will most likely happen. So, again watch what you are thinking. Don't watch the news too often. It has a negative twist on life in general, and 95% are an energy lowering effect on your mind. You don't need that; you need the inverse! You need to laugh, to sing, to dance, and to listen to good energy music all this to elevate your mind and stay connected with Source.

-- In General
When do people really realize what they do have?

Most are healthy, have a decent homes or apartment, eat to their content, Earn enough to get gifts, go to eat out, cloth themselves, have a car, And have a decent life.

--Be aware of your own Limits
There will always be some problems in life, but let us focus on the solutions here...

Do you see what I mean?

The world of infinite possibilities may be shut to you, just because of your beliefs.

<u>Getting ready to Turn Your Life Around</u>

This is the moment to say:

"I re-program myself from average life to winning life.

I think and act like a positive person, and stop acting like a negative person.

This is my moment! I declare that now!

I continue believing in God, Allah, Yaveh, etc. but in a different way.

I think that I must improve my life, starting with this moment!"

NOTES:

_____

_____

_____

_____

_____

Chapter 12
Finding Your Life Purpose

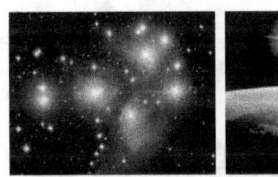

"Stop running after money for a moment. Ask yourself what is your talent, your skill, your passion. This is your True Purpose." Emrick

Finding your life purpose can be tricky for many. Once you find your life purpose, everything will seem to be easy; you will get rewarded for your efforts or non-efforts, because you will not have any problem to align your passion with your purpose in life. Finding purpose in life is very important, because you will offer your expertise, your precious knowledge to many people who are looking for someone who knows what he/she is talking about.

And if you are really good at offering a true knowledge (which is your purpose), people will search for you, will seek you, and will reward you with great generosity, because you made them fulfilled, happy for a moment on stage, and a longer period of time, through your products. Electronic books, audios, videos, or the three of these, seminars, speeches, and webinars are some of the means you can deliver your knowledge. So then, how do you find your life purpose? Here are a few points which can help you just to do that.

Practice:
Finding Your Life Purpose
In 7 Steps

A Turning off all distractions.

Turn off your phone, let the answering machine pick- up, turn off your email alert, and any kind of heavily rhythmic music. Once you have done that, meditate quietly for ten to fifteen minutes, this helping you to clear your mind and your thoughts, so you can be more productive. With a clear mind will you find it easier to write clearly your passion, what your true mission and your purpose are about.

B Listing all the things you would like doing for life.

Go wild in your writing; it is all right. There is no wrong. As you make up your list, write just anything you see yourself doing as your career for at least 4 to 5 years. If you already have a passion, just write it down. It is easier to work on something you will have fun of doing. Why? Because your motivation will always be at its peak when you get yourself ready for doing a business out of it. As multimillionaire Warren Buffet said, "Create value or improve the value in your products."

C Listing all Topics you know Well

Write all which you know enough to talk about it for two to three hours. This is pretty much your favorite topic of conversation you mainly talking about with people, your friends, your spouse, and so on. This is the topic that drives you in a state of passion, which you can harshly make yourself stop of talking about.

D Listing all Subjects in Which You want to Learn more about

Once you have listed your favorite subjects, you will be enthusiastic to proceed and teach others or coach them. This is what is called your "true value.". This is where you will write your topics aligning with your passion, which you will take pleasure spreading around, through teaching with means of speech or writing (in electronic books or short reports). This will give you extra power because since it is your passion, your "drive" you are bound to live your true life purpose.

E List from strongest to lesser strong your skills

List in order or importance in all the skills that you listed on the previous list. Now it is time to take all your lists and write number to each of the items of your lists. It is like to put them in order of importance to you. Take your time doing this. It may be delicate. You mind may start cheating yourself, and you may have problem differentiating between the skills you already have and what you want or wish for having.

F Finding which topic seems to reappear in your lists.

Once you can identify the five skills that are the highest grades, or that made the top of the lists, start writing a sentence containing your reason, your eagerness to practice this skill, unique to you, so you can offer your knowledge to your readers, audience, and/or public. This skill is most usually obtained through research, doing and practice, and reading, than naturally given to you a natural strength.

G Writing Your Mission Statement

Now it is the time, to write your mission statement containing all the qualities and skills you have listed in your top five, as the strongest. This statement, also known as your mission statement, is your purpose in your life. Yes, at this point you already have found your true life purpose, your mission.

Conclusion:

Remember to put your life purpose in a visible place, where you can often see it, and read it. The more you read it and say it, the more your mind is going to work at it, and help you finding all you need to cultivate it, and to deliver to the world the reason why you are here, your true purpose. Each one of us has a purpose. Sadly, many bury their true purpose with excuses such as, "I am not talented enough, there are many who already are doing that, I am too old, too young, too busy," and so on. Wayne Dyer says it very clearly, he says, "Do not die with the music in you." Find you purpose, share your knowledge, and you will make many people happy, and yourself too!

Relationships

"*In a relationship*, there are some stormy moments. We all know that."

A Simple Exercise

Take a pencil and paper, and write about what you like in your spouse or partner.

Just dress up a grocery list.

Do Not write what you don't like!

--I like how you cook

--I like how you arrange and fix up the garden

--I like how you re-arrange the house

--I like your laugh

--I like your class

-- I like your style

-- I like your generosity

-- I like...

You got the idea?

Then read it out loud to yourself,

With emotion and feelings.

Promise yourself you will only see the good in your partner.

Practicing Seeing the Good

Btw, you can also practice seeing the good in others all the time

Many times, people see and focus on what is wrong, fault finders, as Wayne Dyer calls them. You may be a love finder or a fault finder. Just think of that.

You see? Of yes! And then, goes the gossips and blah-blah-blah right?

~~~~~

Meditating to Clear the Mind

It is important to set 15 to 30 minutes a day and meditate. Meditation is crucial because it is like cleaning inside your mind negative and destructive thoughts, or if you prefer it is like clearing a desktop from all kinds of junk both on the desktop, and inside the drawers.

This clearing or cleaning is essential, because your mind cannot function properly if not cleared. If cleared your mind will be ready to fill itself with Love, Creativity, and Abundance. You need these three qualities to accomplish your wishes. Love is for acceptance and consideration for others, who may be able to help you in your projects. Creativity is for any problem or obstacles which could get on your way, as well as how to build, carry on, and finish anything, any project you have your mind on. Abundance is also essential, because it is one of the factors of belief; that nothing will be missing on the puzzle of the project you already have set your mind to achieve, or accomplish.

NOTES:-

_____

_____

_____

_____

_____

_____

_____

_____

_____

_____

Chapter 13
Finding Happiness

"In accepting, in loving, in non-judging, in allowing, in contemplating you will surely find happiness."EG

Happiness is not a pursue in the reality outside of you, but inside your mind. If you carry yourself as a happy human being, everything you want will come your way. That this is almost automatic. To be happy, you must be forgiving.

"Many people in Western culture are striving for success. They want a big home, a successful business, and all these outer things. But doing our research we have found out that having all these outer things doesn't guarantee what we really want which is happiness. So we go for theses outer things thinking they will bring us happiness. But it's backwards. We need to go for the inner joy, the inner peace, and the inner vision first. And then all of the outer things appear."

Marci Shimoff, author.

This quote just speaks for itself; doesn't it?

The Main Happiness Destroyers

Complaining; This is when you say or think, "poor me! I am a victim!"

Blaming others. "It is your fault. You made this happen. It is not my fault!"

And feeling ashamed. "It is all my fault. This is entirely my doing."

Here are some examples of happiness factors called contractions and expansion. The contraction factors are things that undermine your happiness. Here they are:

Contraction   Expansion
You feel guilt or shame   Make peace with yourself
You blaming others, circumstances   look for your lesson
You focus on the problem   Focus on the solution
You react, you feel as a victim...   You respond, you feel you are in control.

Do you feel the difference? Contraction is a state of low energy, prone to attract unwanted experience. On the other hand, the state of expansion invites fortunate experience, elevating events, interesting and fun people. Feel in control of yourself. No one else is, but you. You are the captain of your own life experiences. You are in charge. Start to take controls right now!

Here are more on the Contraction and Expansion feelings and emotions. Just be aware that these feelings guide you towards or away from happiness.

Contraction

Fear
Disappointment, Emptiness
Self-centered,
Sadness, Anger, stress
Resentment, forgiveness

Expansion

Love
Gratitude
Loving Kindness
Sincerity, openness
Forgiveness

Low Energy /High Energy Feelings

Bad feeling: depression k, guilt, resentment, hate, revenge, anger, worry, boredom, annoyance, criticism, blame
Good feeling: love, gratitude, passion, joy, happiness, excitement, joyful expectation, hope, satisfaction

~~~~~~~~~~~~~~~~~~~~~~~~~~~~~~~

The Mirror Exercise

Each time you look at yourself in the mirror, try to say the following feel-good words: "I love you; you are pretty/beautiful/awesome/handsome. You have a caring heart. You are so smart. You are precious to the world. People need you. You are doing your best to help others. You are awesome!"

~~~~~~

Dr. Joseph Murphy said,
"The feeling of wealth produces wealth;
Keep this in mind at all times."

~~~~~~

NOTES: -

_____

_____

Chapter 14:
Tips from a Successful Man,
Jack Canfield

"Energy is everywhere; in your thoughts, your feelings, in all that you see around you." EG

The following is an excerpt re-written from an interview with Jack Canfield. I changed and added some words of my own.

"Everything is Energy!"

"Everything is energy. Each thought you think is an actual request to both the Universe and your subconscious mind. For example whenever you say "I'm sick and tired of something" you really say "I'm sick and tired" and it goes straight to the Universe to give you more opportunities to be both sicker and more tired.

Thoughts are charged with either positive or negative energy. You have to be conscious about that, and aware of how you see the world, as well as how you think.

"What You Think About, You Bring About."

Whatever topic or subject you think about, talk about, focus on , watch on TV, listen over the radio, what you worry about, picture about, anything you give your attention to, you attract more of it to your life. So if you watch any channel news, or continuously negative news, especially news about companies going out of business, one thinks, "Oh no! It is going to be bad for me too!" So when they think about that bad state of affairs, they start attracting this negativity into their own life.

That is why we may have too much information. For instance, there is a recall on a certain type of food, lately it was with eggs. Then we start to be suspicious of all eggs on the market, even though the concern may be for 10% of the total eggs being sold in the markets. Some may start thinking not to buy eggs for a month or so, because of the magnitude of the information being processed by one's mind. This goes for everything; a disaster, an outbreak, a swarm of insects, and so on. It is a good idea not to watch too much the news. Often they exaggerate, and plant negative thoughts in your mind. Try to stick to the headlines, if you want to be still informed about what is going on.

"Match Your Vibration to What You Want."

You cannot receive anything in your life unless your vibration and your energy match to the event, or the object that you wish or want. To get what you want, you must be in a state of abundance, of appreciation or gratitude, because that is the state you would be in if you were to receive something you really want. If I gave you say one million dollars, what state would you be in? You would be in the state of gratitude, of appreciation, you would feel content and secure, and those sorts of feeling. Right?

Your thought and feeling frequency have to be aligned with the Universe.

Vibrations: Like Attracts Like

Like is attracted to like energy. So for example, if you are in a state of abundance, you would attract more abundance in my life. If you would be in a state of high self-esteem, people with high self-esteem would start to come towards you. On the other hand, people with low self-esteem will feel threatened by your presence, or would be afraid to be rejected by you, and they would find other people in the same matching level of self-esteem vibration as them. We all are attracted by a certain kind of personality, which match our level of vibration, our own personality.

Believing in the Universe

So if you are in a state of high self-esteem, certainty, abundance, excitement, enthusiasm expectation, everything is going to work for you. If you believe strongly that it is a beneficial Universe, that God in right by your side, that anything and everything is working out got your best,, you are going to attract a special kind of energy, different sort of people, special kinds of opportunities, than someone who lives in fear, who thinks that things are already bad, and that they will get worse, and so on. Once again, watch and monitor your state of mind, your mood, so you will attract something similar, that match your mood. It is just a question of attitude really.

Taking Responsibility

Every thought you think acts as it if you place an order to the Universe. We all must get 100% responsibility for our thoughts. Where are your thoughts, your attention? Are you focusing on what you want, or on what you are scared about? Remember: whatever you put your attention to, you will to get more.

Life is like a safe with a combination lock. Success is like knowing the correct combination to open it... whenever you get into fear, you cannot remember the code or combination.

Picture this: It is like you were Aladdin and his genius, saying "Your wish is my command." All you have to remember is to order what you want.

How The Universe is like a GPS

All of us have a GPS inside. You do not have to know where you are and where you need to go, to start your trip. You just need to know your destination. The GPS will give you all the directions to get there. The universe is like a GPS. Your job is to know exactly what you wish for. You must get really clear of what you wish, and then you can generate anything that you want. But so many people are not clear on what they wish.

Do not spend time or energy trying to figure out how your wishes are going to come into your life. Just trust the Universe; in time, it will come to you. Sometime faster than other. But it is all right, since you believe, you will receive.

3 TECHNIQUES ABOUT GETTING WHAT YOU REALLY WANT

1. ENERGY DRAINS and OBSTACLES

Irritating objects or malfunctioning objects in your house or living place are energy drains. Take a day, half day, or maybe a couple of hours. Then, go through your home with a note pad or a clip-board, and note anything and everything which you are tolerating, every bit of irritation, anything which is not precisely the way you want. For example; the old screen door, a hole in a wall, a part that needs re-painting, the lose handrail, a mess in your office mess, and so on. Then act on these bits of irritation. You we have to get away from a state of resignation. You have to start to declare, "Yes, I can have anything in my life just the way I want it!"

In the case you we do not act on bits of irritation, you may numb your awareness, with the purpose of not seeing see those objects of annoyance. To do that, you numb out all of your awareness, as well your subconscious ability to come up with creative solutions to your problems. In fact, if you add up little bits of irritation plus other little bits of irritation you end up with a big problem.

2. Starting a Bucket List

Have you watched the movie, "Bucket List?" A great movie; Jack Nicholson and Morgan Freeman... It talks about what follows after writing down a list of wishes to do in one's life. Take a pencil and paper, and write 101 goals you really want to achieve before you die.

If you prefer, you can cut out photos out of periodicals and magazines, what you want to do, to have, to visit. Whatever works best to you.

Once you are done, review your list once a month. Just by reviewing the list, you already start attracting things you want in your life. Why? Because you have decided, you have said to the Universe, "I want this. This is what I really want."

Making a list of what you want is one of the most essential things to do, for your wishes and goals to come about in your reality.

3. __Making Time for Specific Goals__

Take a half day. Then ask yourself what or who do you want to be in 1, 2, 3, 5, years from now.

Then sit down, meditate, for a couple of hours and answer these questions. What do you want to BE in 1, 2, 5 years from now?

Then go to the following 7 categories of your life.

1. __Financially:__ income, cash flow, and so on.

2. __Career:__ what or where do you want to be?

3. __Relationships:__ "I want to have this many friends, this kind of experience with my spouse, live with my perfect soul mate," and so on. **4. __Health /fitness:__** What your level of cholesterol? Run a marathon? **5.** __Fun/Recreation:__ how many vacations do you want to take? Where do you want to go? Do you want to take dancing lessons? Take a theater class?

6. __Personal:__ What are the things you want to own, your spiritual goals,

7. __Contribution:__ What do you want to contribute to society? What is your legacy?

__Honoring your Choices and Preferences__

When you are asking, respect __your__ preferences. Choose what you want for __your__ life. What is the music you love... When you set your goals, you want to consider the things you really want to do, Not "should do."

Some think that they should weight this or that amount, so that people will like them.

As you are working on your goal setting, try to stay away from any idea such as, "what is my spouse going to think about it? What are my friends going to say? What are my colleagues going to tell? And so on. You are setting your goals for your life; what others think about you is none of your business. If you consider too much others opinions, you may doom yourself and not reach your goals so dear to your heart. Think different. Don't worry about them. You will be just fine. Keep focused on your goals.

Don't Set Goals by Your Ego

On the contrary, set your goals with your higher purpose level. To do that, meditate; go deeply inside your mind. Connect with the deepest part of yourself. As a result, you will come up with what you want to achieve in your life. That is why it is important to feel connected to others, your neighbors, and your acquaintances. Remember you are here for a special purpose, and you have a talent that is unique. If you understand that your talent is needed and that people are ready to pay money in exchange for it, you will have whatever you want. "If you give what people want, people will give you whatever you want, and more."

Imagining and Writing Ideal Scenes

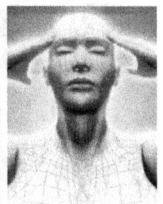

Write ideal scenes for anything you want in your life. Go deeply into your writing. List all the details you can imagine. Use your senses. What would you see, hear, smell, feel, touch, taste. Go into your dream with un-relentless imagination. It is time again to sit quietly, grab a paper and pencil, and write your wishes with all your heart desire. Go wild! Don't stop until you feel you have written all the details that you want. Go on and imagine with all your senses. What you see (color, size, texture), what you hear (soft, loud, noises, music, singing), how it smells (perfume, flavor), how it feels to your touch (rough, smooth, bumpy), how it tastes (flavor, odor, delicate, strong). You will need to add many adjectives there. The more details are the better.

Setting Every Year Your Main Goals

Set every year 21 goals. 3 goals in each area. Then write 250-300 words for each goal. Write the ideal scene.   For instance, "I m so happy and grateful that I am now ....   I am vacationing in .... with a wonderful view on ...... that there is a large pool, and a .... "Write down all the specifics that you want in your ideal vacation.

Dreaming Big!

Dream big, because it takes the same amount of energy to dream big as to dream small. Think big, dream big, believe and receive big stuff! Why, don't you think that is silly to dream of small goals, when it takes the same effort to dream of big goals? It is like to get in the car, drive a mile or two, go to the store and get some milk, instead of getting fruit, vegetables, dessert, water, juice, salt and pepper, and milk.

Asking, "How is My Dream Going to Help Others?"

When you dream about something you want to get in your life, dream not something for you to enjoy, but include others, something that will serve and help others. A dream that will put others in their house of dreams, helping other to achieve their dreams, and so on... There was this real estate agent, whose business was going very slow... one day, she asked herself, "how can I help others?" Then she receives the idea that she would help single mothers to get into their home. Then she had such a success doing that, she started to set up seminars to help single mothers to move into their own houses. Voila!

Building up the Notion of Being of Service

Let's ask, "What is your goal and imagine it." If your goal is just for yourself, your own interest, and someone would ask you to extend your right arm aside, and if the person would push it down, your arm will offer little resistance and just go down. On the other hand, if your goal would be to help, and serve others; your arm would be stronger and it would be almost impossible to push it down.

Your body can be compared to a computer and its tower. You cannot know what happens in your computer unless you can see the display on your monitor, and then you know what program is running, what function you are using, and so on.

Practicing Body Response

In his seminars, Jack Canfield and has his audience standing up. Then he asks "bodies, (Physical bodies) tell me what a Yes answer is." Then most bodies just incline forward (25% of the audience will lean backwards). "Now bodies, show me a No answer." Then, most bodies are going to incline back. At this point, he simply tests them. He says, "My name is Jack Canfield." Bodies would incline lean forward. Then He goes on and asks them to think of something. For instance, he would ask, "Is this for my highest good to pursue this goal you have in mind? For example, to get married? "Then their bodies would give them a yes or no answer, by inclining forward or backward.

BELIEVING

"What the mind can conceive and believe, it can achieve." W. Clement Stone

First you have believed your wish or goal is possible, and then you must take action. If you truly believe that your wish is a done deal, then you let it go to God-Source-Universe. People may call it God, Universe, or Source. If you believe that it is good, that you are aligned in a divine plan, that you are in the flow, and you trust all that, then you can move into action.

How Do We Attract Crime?

An experiment has been conducted with prisoners on the topic of Getting mugged.

Maybe you think that we are not likely to get mugged. Before this experiment, I used to think that the ones who get mugged were truly victims. Jack Canfield used to work with a group of inmates in a prison in New Jersey. There was an experiment conducted there; they were presenting films to violent offenders. Then after the film has been shown to them, they would ask the inmates, "Would you mug that person? -- No, not that one. Yes, that one. Then they would ask "– So what's the difference? –well that person walks with a decided step; they know where they're going. They're the kind of person who would fight back. But that other person has the head down, the shoulders hang down, looking kind of depressed; well, that person looks he doesn't fight back."

So physically, we send out vibrations saying "I'm mug-able. I'm rap-able. I'm rob-able. I'm someone you can push around, you can abuse verbally in a relationship." On the other hand, others are sending out a different kind of vibration, saying in their body language, "don't mess up with me, I know where I stand, don't even think about it."

So if you are in a state of abundance, you are less likely to have this kind of experience of being a victim of a crime, in your life.

So this example illustrates what we can attract. We want to be in a state of "already having" rather than in a state of need, of lack.

These days, people go into fear, into doubt, hopelessness, gloom, depression, even suicide. Why is that? First of all they think and see themselves into the future. They think, "Am I going to lose my job? How about my stocks? I am never going to make it through. I am not going to survive. I am going to lose my house, my job," and so on.

What you want to do is to imagine what you want and feeling the feelings you'd have if already had it. So by me being in a state of abundance, and gratitude, I'm going to attract more, and so on. Now, you're in the state of gratitude. The Universe wants to give you more of what you are grateful for.

"But if I'm in a state of lack, resentful, resigned, bitching and moaning, complaining about how bad my situation is, the Universe is going to give more things I am going to bitch and moan about. I am going to attract more. "

VISUALIZING YOUR GOALS

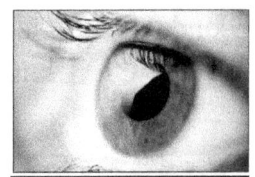

"THIS IS the way to visualize. If you keep visualizing your goals with your vision board add the following word to your vision board: abundance, prosperity, joy, freedom, and other high frequency words.

First, look at the pictures, then close your eyes, and visualize being there, everyday, and feel the feeling of being already there.

"It is not the picture, but the feeling that creates your wish. It is the feeling that you feel once you already have it, that you are there.

For instance, a tennis court. It is the <u>feeling of beating</u> your friends that will produce the tennis court.

In other words, it is the feeling, the emotion you feel as the result of looking at your goal, of focusing on the pictures that generate, create the result, the wish. Also, the main feeling you want to feel is gratitude.

Therefore you want to focus on what you want or wish for, but you want to be in a constant state of gratitude and appreciation on what you already have.

Take a few minutes a day to focus on what you want and then you can release it.

Then the rest of the time, be in a state of vibration, gratitude being the main one.

PRACTICING BEING GRATEFUL

"Right before going to bed, take 5 to 7 minutes and write down what you are grateful for that day. In the evening, tell your spouse what you appreciate about them. Tell them you love them.

"APPRECIATION" BREATHING

"Most of us are out of phase, not in a phase of coherency, where our heart beat and our brain waves are in arrhythmic alignment with each other."

Here is a technique to be in a state of alignment with God-Source, to get in a state of appreciation.

First step, imagine that you are breathing in through your heart,

Close your eyes and focus on your heart. Then imagine that there is an opening, a hole in your chest (imagine a nose, a mouth, a blowhole like a dolphin) where you are inhaling through. Instead of inhaling through your nose or your mouth. Then imagine that you are filling up, loading up, with Love and appreciation. You feel like you are filling up, filling up, and filling up.

"So each time you exhale you heart stays the same, but each time you inhale, it gets larger, bigger. Then you focus on a person or a thing that you really love and appreciate. It can be your spouse, your child, your pet, anything. If you do that for 3 to 4 minutes, you will be in an amazing, euphoric condition. It is nearly hard to believe. Then, while in that overjoyed state ask

God-Source-Universe, "What is the solution to this or that problem?"

Let's say you having trouble with someone at work, or you are Not Manifesting a certain goal you have. Then you ask, "What is it that I need to know, how can I be more effective in handling this situation, or achieving this goal?"

"Then the funny thing is: You will get better answers from your heart than you'll get from your head. Most of us have been taught how to think logically and so on. But when we are in a state of Appreciation, you actually access Deeper Wisdom. This is what many the teachers are teaching these days.

So the feelings of Gratitude and Appreciation are so important.

3 WAYS TO ATTRACT

"These are the ways to attract:
Keeping a journal,
An abundance of appreciation
Appreciate specific people. You may do this by email, phone call, physically, and do the appreciation breathing technique.
These are some ways to create a Vibration Match with the Universe for having anything you want.

Science Experiment with NASA

"There is a student of the law of attraction who has been studying it for a number of years. They found out that we all have an attractor field which extends around our body. NASA conducted an experiment with astronauts. They would pick an envelope labeled with a number, and then they would look inside the envelope and see a shape (a square, circle, triangle, pentagon, etc.) Then they would focus on that shape, for about 3 or 4 minutes, and then they would record it in their log. Meantime at the Para-psychology lab at the University, students would see if they'd pick the same shape as the astronauts, they would close their eyes, go into a receptive mode, they would see what shape would form in their head.

The result is that they would get an uncanny high correlation, accuracy, and way beyond chance. By analyzing the data, now we know that the Speed of Thought, also known as Intention, can travel a minimum of 250,000 miles per sec. This speed of thought can be picked up by machine, but also by people.

STAYING POSITIVE

"It is so powerful and important to stay positive, to stay and be in a state of expectancy.

For example, if you are going to a meeting and do a sales presentation, and if you

Believe, before that meeting, that they are not going to buy anything, you are sending an email, a message through the "Inner

Net" not the internet, and they are receiving something like "don't buy" then you walk in and they already have decided not to buy.

It is also like the dog knowing when the master is heading home. The minute the master is heading home they know. They are picking this up through their inner-net.

So we have to become conscious of the thought we think. That's why the daily disciplines of doing affirmations, doing visualization, monitoring your self-talk, meditating, engaging in these daily disciplines is so critical.

"ONE HOUR EQUALS SEVEN?"

"There is an interesting fact. Researches indicate that one hour of affirmation, meditation, Sedona method, Byron Katie's the work, and such, where you are working on letting go on limiting belief, visualizing what you want, changing your thoughts from negative to positive, meditating on bringing more into your life, like abundance, joy, equals to 7 hours of outer activity in the world. Outer activity is when you work on your own, hard, without any Divine of Universal intervention.

What I noticed, when I started to do this kind of self improvement work, is that instead of a book taking me a year to write, it would take me only a month to write. It is almost as if there was something inside of me, dictating the words, and also that less editing was needed.

A Project: Writing a Book!

Jack Canfield, "You know we came up with the idea of Chicken Soup for the Soul, Mark and I were looking for something we would make a difference in the world , we could also be known, so we could reach more pp, so we could speak to bigger audiences,

The Story of "Chicken Soup for the Soul"

"We wanted to write a bestselling book, and so we said, what would be of a greater service? We said, "Well stories that would inspire and empower people ... and that's how Chicken Soup for the Soul came out as an idea.

And so we didn't have a title, and so we meditated, all week long every day, for an hour, we asked for a title. And then on day 3, I saw a hand on the chalkboard of my mind: Chicken Soup. And then I asked, "Why chicken soup?"And an answer came out, when I was sick as a child, my grandma would give me chicken soup. But why chicken soup? And then the voice came out in my mind and said" pp spirits are sick; they're in resignation, they're in fear," We were in a recession; I got goose bumps, my wife got goose bumps, Mark got goose bumps, my agent got goose bumps,

"We were rejected by 140 publishers. But because we got goose bumps from a higher aspect from consciousness maybe from God, energy, we decided we better stay with this. And then eventually the book got published and sold 100 million copies.

The Inner Work

"This was that inner work, which allowed the outer work to be almost effortless.

That's why dreaming big is so important. Dreaming is closing your eyes, seeing the result, and such a critical part in creating the "Vibration Match." Then what happens is that your attractor field Expands. We've walked into a room where we are attracted to somebody, not by their looks, but by their energy, we just want to get next to them.

Generating "Positive Energy"

"Whenever Robin Williams walks in, we want to go over there, and join him. He's generating so much positive energy.

People do business with people they want to do business with.

And so it's important that you love what you doing, spend time doing what you love, because that raises your attractor field; and this is so important.

Doing What You Love Everyday

"One of the things I teach is to spend a minimum of an hour a day doing what you love. You ought to do that, because you are having too much fun. It may be petting your cat, listening to good music, feeding your animals, we have a barn with horses, chickens, get a massage, play scrabble,

So basically, make a list of 20 things you love to do, and then make sure you're doing one of the things for a minimum of one hour. And what happens is that it creates a vibration of joy. And joy is probably the most important thing other than gratitude and appreciation, which you can ever feel.

And joy is a feedback system. It tells you if you're on course. If you don't feel joy, it is not taking you where you want to go. It is an on-course off-course feedback like sonar.

For example, one student who is a yoga instructor made in one month what she was making in a year. "

<u>Summary</u>

1. Have a vision board. Everyday spend some time looking at it. Insert Words that are 2 to 4 inches wide by 1 inch tall.

2. Read the Key to Living the Law of Attraction.

3. Change your thinking: <u>you need 30 days to change a habit or a belief</u>. You have to do that every day, without skipping one day. (NASA research) 30 days in a row without one miss. So if you do that 16 in a row and you skip day 17, day 18 is day one. You need to start all over."

NOTES:

_____

_____

_____

_____

_____

_____

_____

_____

CHAPTER 15:
Using Clearing Methods

Using the Power of Releasing
For Money Affirmation

"Money is really nothing but energy. It is really a form of exchange, a way to thank. Also it is not a goal by itself. It is a mean to a goal."

When you are doing your money affirmations or other affirmations, often times you become aware of some competing limiting belief thoughts, for instance:

You are dreaming! You are kidding yourself! Who are you kidding?

You are never going to get rich! That's too simple!

You must have extra cash to make real money!

When this happens, take a seat, grab a paper and pencil, and write your or one of these limiting belief thoughts or objections down. Then, close your eyes and release the previous thoughts and feelings or emotions included in these.

A Clearing Technique: The Sedona Method

Here is another straightforward technique for releasing limiting beliefs.

It is called the Sedona Method, as a part of training by Hale Dwoskin. Several Law of Attraction Masters and Success coaches recommend taking his seminar and reading his book, the Sedona Method by Hale Dwoskin. He also offers to the public the Sedona Method Home Study, that you can find on the internet at www.sedona.com

A Basic Releasing Method

As you go about with your affirmations, and any limiting belief is coming in ["haunting you in-"] your mind, your first reaction is naturally tending to ignore, suppress, or resist these limiting thoughts or emotions. Unfortunately, this keeps them in your mind! What you have to do, is to let your mind completely experience the associated feeling or emotion and then release them.

Most people state that closing their eyes help them to be more centered on their feelings or emotion.

Here is the process that you can take, when you have a negative or limiting money related thought coming up to your mind.

Question 1: "What is my feeling, at this moment?"

Concentrate on what emotion or feeling you feel as you experience a limiting negative thought or belief about money comes up to you.

Question 2: "Can I welcome it?"

Simply welcome the negative or limiting feeling or emotion.

Question 3: "Could I let it go?"

Here, you choose an answer: yes or no.

Question 4: "Would I let it go?"

Ask this to yourself. Are you prepared, willing, and ready to let this feeling of emotion go?

Question 5: "When?"

Ask yourself that question. Letting go is your own decision, which you can take anytime. You can answer this question with: Now!

"Lather, Rinse, Repeat"

Then simply repeat this process as much as you need, until you are free of your limiting or negative feeling or emotion, associated with your affirmation.

NOTES:

_____

_____
_____
_____
_____
_____
_____
_____
_____
_____

Chapter 16
Using Affirmation Tips

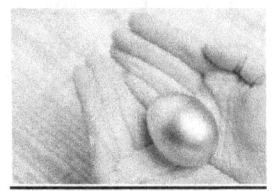

After each affirmation, say with conviction, I do deserve this or that.

<u>No attachment to the outcome</u>.

Do not be attached to the outcome, otherwise, it creates a state of lack, of need. This state blocks the affluence of your wishes.

Forget about the outcome, which means be detached.

From time to time put away some picture from your vision board and replace them with something else you want to manifest.

<u>Trust the universe.</u>

Trust the Universe your wishes will come at the "right time.

Raise your vibrations by being happy, laugh, go dance, do something you love doing.

<u>Be grateful</u>

Thank god or the Universe for what is coming, your wishes of course.

<u>Get passionate</u>

Each morning, start with thanking god-source-universe for what you have your possessions, your situation physical and health, and the good experiences in your life.

Power of Fear

Fear is a destroyer of your attracting power. Acknowledge and analyze fear, and fear goes away. What you resist persists. This feeling or emotion is too underrated. Many people have fear, which causes stress, which causes many illnesses and sometimes even death. A majority of the Masters of the Law of Attraction and success coaches agree on the following: the opposite of Love is Fear. One would have tendency to put hate as the opposite, but it is not. Our primal feelings or emotions are Love and Fear. From Love stem out a quantity of secondary emotions, and from Fear also, a considerable number of secondary feelings stem out of it. Among them, hate. Love attracts; Fear repels, pushes back.

Wisdom Words: A Tale

"Which Wolf Do You Feed?"

Here is a Cherokee Story. Once there was a man who ask a Shaman, "What is the Secret for Happiness?" the Shaman thought and told the man the following story. "Inside of us there are two wolves. One was Unhappiness including Fear, Worry, Jealousy, Anger, Self-Pity, Sorrow, inferiority, and resentment. The other wolf is Happiness including Love, Hope, Joy, Serenity, generosity, kindness, Truth and Compassion." Then, the man turned to the Shaman and asked, "--Which wolf wins? –- The one you feed."

Which wolf are you feeding?

It is a fact: happy people are cheerful and have kindness, support, and encouragement in their attitude and behavior to themselves. Their thinking about themselves is full of love and compassion.

Another Wise Story

BEAUTY

A man comes to see the Master and asks "--Why everyone is so happy?

The master answers "Because they learned how to see Goodness and Beauty everywhere they are. – But why don't I see

Beauty and Goodness all around? – Because you cannot see outside what you cannot see inside of you."

__What is Your Purpose?__

You were brought in this world to create, love, be kind, and express beauty in your own way. You cannot attract pleasant appearance in your life by hating anything about you.

You attract what you radiate. You must raise the energy that you want to attract: the happiness you want, the love you miss, the abundance you crave. If you criticize the absence of these feelings, you will attract conflict and criticism to your life.

Wisdom

NOTES:

_____
_____
_____
_____
_____
_____
_____

Chapter 17
Looking at Aspects of the Law of Attraction

"Nothing happens until something moves."
Albert Einstein

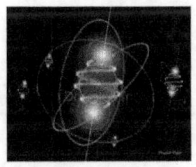

The "High Energy Effect"

An interesting fact is that higher or faster energy has an impact on lower or slower energy: it annihilates it, it dissolves it. That is why it is so crucial to have the habit of visualizing, praying or meditating, and feeling good. People who have a great amount of positivity or high energy, such as the Dalai Lama and such, can counter balance negative energy of millions of people. That is how powerful high energy is. This is really good news, because these high energy people give balance to our world. Also high energy thoughts are more powerful that lower energy thought. That is also good news for your system of thought, which you can alter and modify for your own good.

Energy and Its Various Forms

Here is a series of energy in its different forms. As you can see, it has different properties and qualities.

The energy vibrations, or vibes, can be felt. You feel them sometimes. That is why you may say about this about a person, he/she has bad vibes. It is entirely explained in the analysis of the energy field.

The Physical Energy

In the physical or material world, the energy is in its solid form state; it is energy in its slow state. The harder the material, the more compacted and slow is the energy property.

The Sound and Noise Energy

The energy in the sound world is much faster than the physical energy. Speed: 1000 meters per second. The sound wave of the note A is of 440 Hz or vibrations per second. It is not visual, but can be felt. Have you noticed how a loud drum can literally hit your chest and your eardrums?? In the following example, we will pay particular attention to the mantra effect of energy. The Mantra, through the sound level emitted can connect your energy and aligns it to God-Source-Universe. Through the practice of mantra, the sounds of Ohm and Ah have this property of connection. The Ah sound is common through the naming of God-Source-Universe. To hear it, say the following words: God, Allah, Buddha, Krishna, and Rama. Did you hear it? You can practice this sound in your daily meditation time.

The Thought Energy

Much faster energy than the sound energy. Through an experiment, it has been concluded that the [positive] thought speed was about 250,000,000 meters per second. Very high frequency also. It is slightly slower than the light energy, but picture that: your prayer and meditation are just a little slower than light! Now keep in mind that thoughts can be high energy or low energy loaded. You want to keep your thought on the high energy level. You know, Love, Happiness, Joy, Compassion, Hope, Serenity, generosity, kindness, and such.

The Light Energy

The light energy is faster than the thought energy. Speed of light: 300,000,000 meters per second. You already know that, when you see someone hitting a ball in the distance, you first see the ball being hit, and then you hear the sound. In another example, the thunder is slower to reach you than the flash of the electrical and visual thunderbolt. Also, red is slower than the color violet: that is why we call them infra-red and ultra-violet. Remember the power of the ultra-violet on your skin? We don't warn anyone of the infra-red power. Note: The beauty of light is that it travels fast in the darkness. A candle light in the deepest night can be seen from miles away.

A Word About Matter

Max Planck, Nobel Prize winner, upon receiving his honor, said, "After studying matter all my life, here is my conclusion: There is No matter as such. All matter originates and exist only by virtue of a force which brings the particles of atoms to vibration and hold this micro system of atoms together. Behind this force is a conscious intelligent mind, the Matrix of All Matter."

NOTES:_____

_____

_____

_____

_____

_____

_____

_____

_____

Chapter 18:
Your INNER DIALOGUE

"You cannot remedy anything
by condemning it"
Wayne Dyer

Monitoring Your Inner Voice

At all times, monitor your little inner voice, the one that criticizes. Be careful when it focuses on the past, on the negative thoughts about people and life events, on what is missing, and on others opinions and gossips.

Say "I focus my mind to attract what I want and stop thinking about what is do not want."

View obstacles and challenges in your life as opportunities, or lessons to be learned. See yourself in these situations as an observer, not a victim. Remain in control of your life.

Sending Away Doubt

When doubt is cast out, banished, abundance will increase and anything becomes possible. Even though you see nothing that shows that you are realizing your wish in your life, refuse to think about doubt. If you do that, you doubt God-Source-Universe and nothing that you want will come to reality, but just panic or fear.

The Good Habits About Self-Talk

1. Keeping track of your Inner-Voice

Be aware of how your inner voice focuses on what is missing, the negative news, negative gossips, negative ideas and criticizing, and judging, the past, and others opinions. Change all that from "I resent that I am missing ..." to something like, "I aim to attract what I want and I stop thinking of whatever I dislike."

2. Seeing Obstacles as Opportunities

Tell yourself, "I aim to remain connected to God-Source, no matter what, and increase my power from the Universe.
I am an observer no more a victim."

As you say that, with more and more trust and belief, you will see your dreams take shape, come to your reality almost like by magic.

You will also influence others, by creating ripples of positive energy around you.

3. Doing This In Times of Depression and Doubt

Have faith in God-Source-Universe. Have you taken the plane? The Sun is always, always shining above the clouds. And when it rains, there is often a rainbow to be seen. There is always hope. Sometimes, just be patient, and wait with positive expectation, with knowing that your wish is coming. Do not try to rush anything. Be and rest assured that the solution to your problem is on its way. God-Source never, never says No. He/She always says Yes. Because He/She loves you.

Saying Affirmations

**"I love myself and appreciate who I am.
I am whole and perfect because I am created by
"Whole and Perfect."
I respect and appreciate others.
I love others no matter what.
I refrain from judging others, because it creates
separation.**

I say to myself and others,
"I belong Here and Now!"
I am never alone, because my Creative Partner is with me always.
I meditate to always be connected to God-Source.
I love my enemies, and I forgive them.
I know that if I doubt or punish me, I attract
More doubt and poor opinion to me, which is more punishment.
I am always in a state of gratitude.
Thank You"

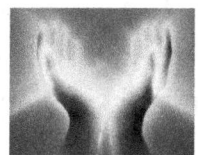

<u>A Message from God</u>

"Good Morning.
This is God.
I will be handling all
Your problems today.
I will not need your help,
So have a miraculous day."

NOTES:

_____

Chapter 19
PRACTICING THESE GOOD HABITS

"A habit is a way of life. If you want to change your life, you have to adopt a new set of habits."Unknown

We all have heard this: To be in top shape, exercise and eat healthy food. A healthy mind in a healthy body. Yes, these are true. So, "get on your horse" and start practicing the following simple changes.

Controling Your Body and Mind

Practice healthy, non-toxic patterns or habits. For instance, stop watching the news, those negative talk shows, people's court programs, and/or unconstructive soap operas. Instead, go and take a long bath with scented salts and scented candles or oil lamps, in a dim lighting. Or go to your backyard or the park and meditate or just plainly contemplate the nature surrounding you.

Eating healthy food

If you do, stop eating junk food, high in chemicals, high in fat, high in sugar, high in corn syrup (the worst form of sugar) , and low in natural ingredients, low in minerals and vitamins, and the truly good nutrients. Take the habit of reading the label on the food you buy, and be discriminatory of "junk" ingredients.

Exercising

It is good to exercise every day. But if you don't have the time to go to the gymnastic club, go for a walk for 30 minutes. You can take your dog for a walk too, if you have, or your tamed tiger if you prefer. While exercising, picture positive mental images of you being in a top shape; this will accelerate the effects of exercising benefits.

Meditating

I cannot emphasize enough the benefits of meditation. It just keeps you in alignment with God-Source-Universe, and fills you up with positive energy, and clears you out from bad energy. You, as everybody nowadays, have an overload of information, and it is something you need to clean your mind on regular basis. This information can be through talks, advertisements, and so on. Just be aware of that overload of information, and clear your mind.

Practicing Wisdom

Be patient. Stop getting upset, and Do not take yourself so seriously.

There are two things we have in mind. Education and Wisdom. Wisdom does not get much focus nowadays. It is highly under-rated. But if you become wise, you become in alignment with God-Source-Universe.

Surrendering, Giving In

Submit to God-Source, and Let go.

When the going gets tough, remind yourself that you have a mission and a silent partner who is always by your side.

Act as if your wishes are already achieved, as if you are already who you want to become.

An Additional Personal Note
About Books, Movies, Music

Reading, Movie Watching, Music listening; all these activities trigger our mind and emotions.

On this topic, just use your own judgment. What you read either enriches you with positive emotions or delivers negative feelings. Movies that you watch have basically the same effect. I don't say you should not see any action movie, such as Armageddon, I just say that some movies don't leave you with a good message or feeling, but with some fear, or anger, and so on , which in turns lower your energy. Even the kind of music you listen to can trigger a positive or negative charged vibration or energy frequency. I stay away from violent and shocking lyrics as much as possible. I would say, look into these media with a wise judgment. Try to find enrichment rather than non-enriching movies, books, and music and songs.

Listening to Classic Music and Opera

One experience to live is to go to a classic concert or to the opera. There are great array emotions, which can figuratively transport your soul higher than you ever could imagine.

Everything carry Positive or Negative Vibrations

There is an experiment, where an object triggers a positive or negative emotion to the mind. David Hawkins writes about how he could even calibrate from an energy gauge which ranges from 10 to 1,000. Each emotion is triggered by circumstance. Each object can deliver low or high energy. For instance if you were to pick a violent DVD or CD recording and hold it close to your heart, and you would extend your arm sideways, and someone else would come and press your arm, there would be very little resistance , and your arm would go down easily , without much pressure. On the other hand, if you would hold to your heart something which contains more positive energy, such as a Mozart record, the other person would have much more to do to press your arm and make it go down. To know more about this, I recommend reading <u>Power vs. Force by David R Hawkins</u>.

NOTES:

_____

_____

_____

_____

_____

_____

_____

_____

_____

Chapter 20
Raising Your Energy

"Energy can be high or low. You have the power to raise your energy at all time. Just be aware of it. Be conscious of it, often. " EG

Collecting Photos

Find photos taken in moments of pure happiness and joy, kind feelings, love, and in the zone of receptivity. Then put these photos around your house or home; on the fridge, on your vision board, around your desk, and so on. These photos carry positive, high energy and radiate it to you.

Energy, Friends, and Relatives

Be aware of what kind of energy comes from your friends, and relatives. Try to select people who are with good and high energy levels, which will empower you. Try to stay in contact with the one who are truly seeing your values and show you appreciation, who can feel and tell your greatness. When you are in their energy field, your anger, doubt, depression, and fear will just dissipate.

Empowering Activities

As often as you can, go to hike in the nature, or go camping, or go fishing. This will keep your energy level very high and you will feel the connection to God-Source-Universe.

Also try to go and take yoga classes, attend lectures or seminars, get a massage (recommending: Chinese foot massage). Go and visit spiritual place with meditation centers (e.g., Self-Empowerment Fellowship, Eastern Temples. Also recommenced: to go and visit sick children and old people in hospitals and convalescent homes. This is to cultivate compassion, which raise your energy and Universal connection.

Practicing "RAK"
Random Act of Kindness

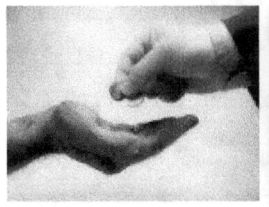 

Practicing Random Acts of Kindness will also raise your energy level. Of course, you can give a dollar to a street man, but that is not enough. Send him a silent blessing; smile with a kind smile (not a smile full of pity!); tell him some nice words, like "Here you are. Good luck to you; Do not despair; Keep faith; you are not alone."

<u>Saying Affirmations:</u>
<u>Some examples</u>

I aim to attract the career I want in my life.

I aim to attract the love of my life.

I aim to attract and afford this car, and I Envision me driving it by the 30th of ... (name a month).

I aim to donate two or three hours to the poor, this month.

I aim to heal me of this constant tiredness.

I aim to attract living in this mansion by the 30th of ...

Thank you,

God-Source-Universe

NOTES:

_____

_____

Chapter 21
How We See the World

"The world is not really as it is; it is as you see it. If you want to change your life, just change the way you see everything."EG

Abundant World

The world is abundant. The Universe is also abundant. The world is a friendly place. If you are having problem believing this, maybe it is time for you to go to the park and see how people are acting, the care and the love that is all around. I say the park, but it can be the terrace of a café, or restaurant, or any other public place. Yes, the world is a friendly, abundant, loving place.

State of Allowing

You have to stay in a state of allowing.

Use the present tense and the word Now to be aligned with God-Source-Universe. Act as if you are already living in abundance and success. E.g., go and buy yourself the higher end of a product, or do and treat yourself with a nice meal, or go and get a Chinese foot massage, or ...

Know that your Prosperity and Abundance will do good to others.

Watching your Feelings

Keep an eye on your feelings to keep connected to God-Source-Universe. If you feel good, keep doing what you are doing. Feel feelings such as Bliss and Passion, as you go along living your life. Be as generous with your fortune to others as the Universe is to you. Stay away from owning or hoarding whatever you get, you receive from God-Source.

Be Grateful

Expand and grow a gratitude attitude for anything that shows up in your life or manifests itself. For example, the moments of Joy, Happiness, being in the Zone, feeling so alive, feeling on purpose, or aligned with God-Source –Universe.

Seeing Your Ego and You

Ego, the low energy that is either dormant and almost absent or active, attracts Stress and Anxiety in your mind. In fact Ego is entirely creating them! There is no per-se Stress and Anxiety in the world.

Ego tells you, "It is better to be right than to be Happy. I must win, because winning is everything to me. Success is all about accumulating possessions and wealth for me, rather than feeling blessed and Happy." And so forth.

Saying Affirmations

I attract success and abundance to me,
Because that is who I am.
I want to feel good (if others question your beliefs).

~~~~~~~~~~~~~~~~~~~~~~~

NOTES:

_____

_____

_____

Chapter 22

HIGH ENERGY DIET

"You are what you eat. Food should be examined to bring nutrients to your vehicle: your body."

You must be careful of what you eat and put into your body. Remember, a sound mind exist by virtue of a healthy body.

Here are a few ingredients that are good, filled with high energy for you:

Fruits, vegetables, grains, nut, soy (in any form), virgin olive oil.

The following are bad, or filled with lower energy:
Ice cream, candy bars, sugar filled food, and corn syrup is <u>very</u> bad, red meat, white flour as in white bread.

Key factors to a High Energy Diet

- ☐ Avoid all refined sugars, e.g., white sugar, and refined honey.
- ☐ Instead, eat brown sugar, and raw honey, or Blue Agave Syrup.
- ☐ Avoid refined carbohydrates such as white bread, biscuits, cakes, white rice, and other processed foods. Read the label.
- ☐ Instead, eat multigrain breads, whole wheat bread, and such.
- ☐ Avoid coffee, black tea, and cigarettes. Limit drinking <u>alcohol</u>.
- ☐ Instead, drink green tea, and herbal teas.
- ☐ Eat abundantly vegetables, raw or barely cooked— eat as a minimum four servings a day.
- ☐ Have three pieces of <u>fresh fruit</u> a day.
- ☐ Eat more legumes such as, lentils, beans, nuts, seeds, and whole grains.
- ☐ Eat more fresh fish.

In is much recommended to eat (non-processed) fresh fish and free-range chicken instead of red meats. Also try to drink plenty of water (recommended: 64 ounces per day = half-gallon = 8 glasses), herb teas or non sweetened or lightly sweetened fruit juices. If you keep eating these types of healthy foods as your high energy <u>diet</u>, you will maintain sufficient blood sugar levels for consistent energy, and avoid the peaks and troughs in blood sugar levels caused by consuming <u>too much sugar</u>. If you prefer, the sugar high then sugar crash you may experience when you do not eat healthy. This kind of up and down in your energy may stimulate the release of stress-related <u>hormones</u>.

With this high energy <u>diet</u>, when you eat is as much important as what you eat. The most important meal of the day is <u>breakfast</u>. Do not skip breakfast or have a cup of coffee and a piece of toast. What you eat for breakfast decides how you will <u>feel</u> for the rest of the day for that matter. It is a mistake to eat so soon, right after waking up, since your <u>digestive system</u> is not yet completely functioning. If you start your day with about fifteen minutes of light exercise, such as jumping jacks or stretching, your appetite will move into action, then your energy level will be at best performance.

NOTES:_____

_____

_____

_____

_____

_____

_____

_____

****

Chapter 22
Last Thoughts

**"Helping others is something we always have
Inside of us. Let us not deny ourselves
of this precious gift." EG**

Contemplating your surroundings

Viktor E. Frankl, (Viktor Emil Frankl) M.D., Ph.D., psychologist
and author, and Austrian neurologist and psychiatrist as well as a
Holocaust survivor, said that , even being a prisoner, he could find

beauty in everything he looked at; he contemplated anything and everything. Can you imagine his surroundings? He was probably surrounded by wooden and barren walls, barracks, no flowers, simple plain clothes, dirt on the floor, and dirt outside, fellow underfed prisoners, soldiers in their strict face and uniforms, and so on. Nevertheless, he found beauty in the midst of this plain, depressing world. Thanks to God-Source-Universe, you are not there.

Looking for Beauty

If you want, go to the park, the supermarket, a Museum, anywhere you need to go, and contemplate. That means look for the beauty in your environment. Look for the positive things and expressions on the face of the people and children. Look at life with the passion of someone who may die tomorrow. Drink life's beauty and realize how life is full of treasures. Don't rush in any place you go through, but try to be a magnet of good feelings, and see the positive things there are always to see.

<u>Cultivating Positivity</u>

Remember, even in the confine of the gloomiest surroundings, Viktor Frankl found beauty. Actually, he was so positive in his view of life, that he treated he fellow prisoners and infused his positivity in their mind. That is the power of positivity.

Passing on Your Energy

Now this is something you need to know. You are energy. Whenever or wherever you are, you carry that energy in you and even all around you. You can pass on this energy to everyone around you. Remember though that you need to keep your energy to a high, and avoid to get stuck in the low energy. Your energy creates and energy field, which is transmitted to your surroundings and as you know now, to the Universe. The way you think, or judge, affect this energy. The way you talk, or show your body language (without talk), the expression on your face, and of course your words and actions affect the people surrounding you. Make a habit of paying compliments or saying nice words to people you meet, such as cashiers, employees, and so on. You will first feel good for yourself, and also make them feel good.

You, Having a Mission

You have a mission. Find your mission. Your mission is in your talent(s). I believe we all are here to make this world a better place.

Gandhi said, "Be the change you want to see." So if you make a mistake, correct it as quickly as possible, so you and feel good in your heart, (and feel the Divine, God-Source in your mind). Appreciate even the faintest improvements, the littlest, trivial niceties in your life, a smile, a laugh, anything. And by magic, you will feel good, in touch with the Universe, and your life will change beyond your best expectations.

"You can begin right now to feel prosperous, to feel healthy,
to feel the love that is surrounding you, even if it is not there.
And what will happen is that the Universe will correspond to
the nature of your song. The Universe will correspond to that
inner feeling,
and manifest because that is the way you are feeling."
Dr. Michael Beckwith

Do you see now the power you have in you? Yes you have this power to transform your life beyond your wildest dreams! So be excited, because you are already changing your life, starting now! Go ahead and do the practice exercises, be thankful, give and receive, be in the flow, and miracles are going to bloom around you like a magic garden, your garden, with flowers you have created.

~~~~~~~~~~~~~~~~~~~~~~~~~~

Food for Thought...

Where are we in LIFE EXPECTANCY?

Comparing Life in the US with the world
Many countries in Africa have a life expectancy to
Between 39 and 56 yrs
In the US: number 20 in the world, 79.4 yrs
Japan at 82.6 yrs

Talking about EARNINGS

If you earn $20K, you are in the top 11.16% richest pp in the
world!
30K → 7.16%
40K → 3.17%
50K → 0.98%
Source: http://www.globalrichlist.com/

WOW!

http://my.opera.com/wertum/blog/index.dml/tag/population

Fact: If the World Population was reduced to 100...

If the world's population could be reduced to a village of 100 inhabitants and at the same time keep the proportion of people who exist on the planet, the village would consist of: 57 Asians, 28 European,14 Americans (both continents),8 Africans.

Since it would be:

52 women and 48 men,30 white and 70 other races; 89 straight and 11 homosexual men,

6 rich men who own 59% of all wealth and all would be from the

U.S.,80 of them live in miserable homes,
70 of them would be illiterate person,
50 of them would not have enough to eat and suffered from the shortcomings, 1 would be dying while 1 was born,1 of them would have a computer, and only 1 would have a university degree.

If you see the world so, then obviously you appreciate your own life as a single. It is nice if you think so - and so take this into account:

1. If you woke up this morning more healthy than sick - you are happier than millions of people that would not survive next week!

2. If you have never been in the middle of a war threat; if you are not alone in prison, if you have not experienced the agony of torture or not starving - you are happier than 500 million people on the planet!

3. If you are free to go to church or mosque, and that no one is threatening you, torturing or killing - you have better luck than 3 billion people!

4. If you have food in your refrigerator, if you are dressed decently, if you have a roof over your head or have somewhere to sleep - you are richer than 75% of the population on the planet!

5. If you have money in the bank or your wallet - you will not believe it, but you are one of the 8% of people with the highest privilege in the world!

6. If your parents are still alive in marriage - you're really rare person !

7. And if you read this message, you receive a double blessing: first, that someone thought of you, and that you are not one of the 2 billion people who are illiterate!

Here's Another Message:

- Smile!
- Live as if you live in "paradise" on earth!
- Meet others with an open mind.
- If you do not, nothing good will happen.
- But if you do, someone will smile thinking of you.
- Is that for you was not enough for comfort and morale?
- What would you do more for others?
- You are now starting to feel happy!

About the author

Because of experiences in my life, I became interested in the subject of the Law of Attraction, also known as the Law of Creation. I studied it intensely for 9 years, and have acquired a solid knowledge in the field. I researched it and interviewed life coaches. My nature has always been to help others. I took this from a great man whom I regret only one thing: to have lost him at a very young age. He was my grandfather.

He liked helping people around, and had many talents: magic, composing music, drawing nature after life, and achieved a variety of different projects. I remember him making entirely from scratch a puppet theater, with characters, and even an entire script to entertain the children of the village where he retired. Most of the things he did were with one aim: to help people feel good, to have people have a good time, to raise the energy of those around him. He was a great humanist. I hope to be remembered as he is. I dedicate this book in his memory.

Resources

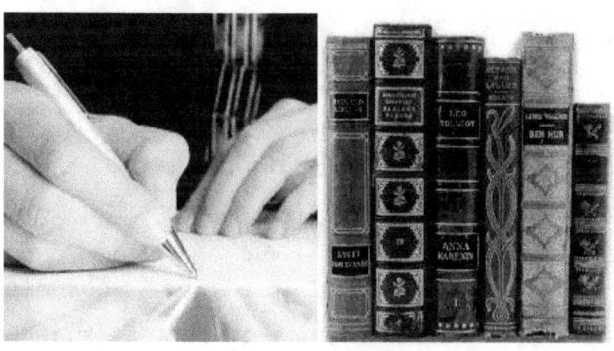

Recommended Speakers

Rev. Michael Beckwith
Les Brown
Lisa Nichols
Jack Canfield
Viktor Hansen
Wayne Dyer
Marci Shimoff
Hale Dwoskin
Brian Tracy
Tony Robbins

<u>Sources</u>

The Success Principles, by Jack Canfield
Interview with Jack Canfield by David Riklan
Sedona Method, by Hale Dwoskin
Happy For No Reason, by Marci Shimoff
The Secret, by Rhonda Byrne
The Power of intention, by Wayne Dyer
Power vs. Force, by David R. Hawkins
I'm Rich Beyond My Wildest Dreams , by Thomas Pauley

Recommended Websites

Free eBook gift by Joe Vitale	www.attractmoneynow.com
Sedona Method at	www.sedona.com
Free guided Meditations	www.just-a-minute.org
Self Improvement Community	www.selfgrowth.com
Jack canfield	*http://www.jackcanfield.us//about/*
Jack Canfield	*www.jackcanfield.com*
Jack Canfield	*www.thesuccessprinciples.com*

Also

www.agapelive.com

www.artofliving.org

www.drdemartini.com

www.emofree.com

www.lefkoeinstititue.com

www.lindwallreleasing.org

www.greatfuleness.org

www.changelimitingbeliefs.com

www.thepassiontest.com

www.kundalinicare.com

www.intentionalhappiness.com

www.innermagician.com

www.soulmatekit.com

www.springforestgigong.com

www.vedicsky.com

www.thework.com

www.goodmorningworld.org
www.happinessclub.com
www.bobproctor.com
www.bobproctorcoaching.com
www.thesgrprogram.com
www.sixminutestosuccess.com
www.selfgrowth.com
www.michaelbox.net
www.commongroundfellowship.com

Recommended Readings/Books

Hale Dwoskin,	the Sedona Method
Marci Shimoff,	Happy for No Reason
Deepak Chopra,	The Seven Spiritual Laws of Success
Dr. Wayne Dyer,	the Power of Intention
Jack Canfield,	The Key to Living the Law of Attraction
Jack Canfield,	The Success Principles
Joe Vitale,	The Attractor Factor
Joe Vitale,	Life's Missing Instruction Manual
Joe Vitale,	The Key: Missing Secret for Attracting Anything You Want
Nan Akasha,	Already Rich
Dr. David R Hawkins,	Power Vs. Force
Rhonda Byrne ,	the Secret
Lynn Grabhorn,	Excuse Me, Your Life is Waiting

Doreen Banaszak, Excuse Me, Your Life is Now

Paul McKenna,   Change Your Life in 7 days

Brian Tracy,   Goals

Deepak Chopra The Seven Spiritual Laws of Success

Deepak Chopra The Spontaneous Fulfillment of Desire

Wayne Dyer   The Secrets to Manifesting Your Destiny

Wayne Dyer   10 Secrets for Success and Inner Peace

Wayne Dyer   Manifest Your Destiny: the Nine Spiritual Principles

Mark Victor Hansen The One Minute Millionaire, Enlightened Way to Wealth

Thomas L. Pauley   I'm Rich Beyond My Wildest Dreams

Daniel D. Amen,   A Magnificent Mind at Any Age

Movies to Watch

Here is a list of movies picked for their inspiration, purpose, and wisdom. Enjoy!

Conversations with God

The Peaceful Warrior
The Secret
What the Bleep? Down the Rabbit Hole
Sea biscuit
The Spirit of St Louis
Mr. Smith Goes to Washington
Searching for Bobby Fisher
Mr. Deeds Goes to Town
Young Mr. Lincoln
It's a Wonderful Life (by Frank Kapra)
The Bucket List
As Good As It Gets
Gandhi
Invictus
The Gift
The Notebook
The Note
Seven Years in Tibet
Remember Me
Phenomenon
Powder

~~~~~~~~~~~~~~~~~~~~~~~

Now, it is time to say Goodbye.
I hope, to have made an impact in your life.
May you live in a transformed
Life with a positive energy
And bring to the world a treasure
You have forgotten for so long:
You! with your long awaited talents!

Love and Happiness to You,
Always,

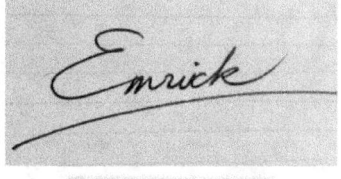

Cherish the Secrets from this book.

Pass on the Secrets of this book.

Thank You

Namaste

~~~~~~~

~~~~~

~~

www.bestyourlife.com
www.EmrickGaram.com

☐ Please consider the environment before printing this. Thank you.